Active Grammar Exercises

D. Adamson
D. Cobb

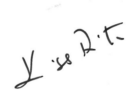

Longman

Longman Group UK Limited
Longman House, Burnt Mill, Harlow,
Essex CM20 2JE, England
and Associated Companies throughout the world

First published 1987
This book accompanies the English monolingual edition of
Active Grammar, published by Longman Group UK Ltd in
1986, which is based on the bilingual edition of the same title
published by Langenscheidt-Longman in 1984.

Acknowledgements

We are grateful to the following for permission to reproduce
the following copyright photographs:
BBC Hulton Picture Library for pages 96 (top right) & 97
(middle left & bottom right); Camera Press Ltd for pages 89
(top left), 96 (bottom right) & 97 (bottom left); The J. Allan
Cash Photolibrary for page 89 (bottom left); Hull City Council
for page 89 (middle left); Island Navigation Corporation Ltd
for page 89 (middle right); Popperfoto for pages 88 (bottom)
& 97 (top right); Topham Picture Library for pages 88 (top),
89 (top right & middle) & 97 (top left & middle right); United
States Travel Service for page 89 (bottom right).

Illustrated by David Parkins, Peter Dennis, Ed McLachlan,
Geo Parkin, Jane Lydbury, Pat Tourret and Hardlines.

Set in Helvetica Light and Medium
Printed in Great Britain
by Mackays of Chatham, Kent

ISBN 0 582 51739 7

Contents

Foreword

Foreword

Active Grammar Exercises gives practice in the main areas of English grammar up to intermediate level. It can be used to practise the grammatical points covered in *Active Grammar*, but can also be used in conjunction with other grammars, or even on its own.

The exercises are suitable for students who have recently been taught the various grammar points. There is also material suitable for students who already have some command of English – and may even have good oral fluency and comprehension – but who need revision to improve their grammatical accuracy. Some exercises focus on single forms, while others focus on the distinctions between two or more forms, and the meanings which give rise to these distinctions. The exercises which contrast various forms are also useful for finding out areas of grammar which students may be weak in.

The points covered in the exercises are set in a situational and language context throughout, often within continuous texts. This helps the student to recognize the meanings and communicative intentions bound up with the choice of one grammatical form rather than another.

As well as being suitable for use in class, the exercises can be used by students working on their own, with the help of the *Answer Key*, which is provided separately.

The index to the exercises resembles that of the companion *Active Grammar* and the headings to the exercises include the numbers of the corresponding sections of *Active Grammar*. These sections will help in doing the exercises, and it is therefore desirable to work through them beforehand. This applies to both students in class and students working on their own.

Section one:

The simple sentence

1. Kinds of subject (1.1.2)

Underline the subjects in this conversation.

Example:
Grand Motorbike Sale begins tomorrow!

Linda: I'm going to buy a motorbike.
Andy: That will be fun! My friend Steve bought one last month.
Linda: You and Steve can come to the shop and help me, if you like.
Andy: OK. Choosing the right bike isn't always easy. Some bikes look good, but they don't always go so well.
Linda: To choose the best bike often takes time. Once my mother spent a whole day buying a dress!
Andy: What sort of bike are you going to buy?
Linda: Dad says a 250cc bike will be big enough.
Andy: Your father's probably right.

2. Kinds of object (1.1.3)

Underline the objects in this advertisement.

Example:
Everyone can help the hungry people of the world.

Did you know people buy 1,500,000,000 drinks in aluminium cans each year? And that aluminium is worth a lot of money? So, when you finish your drink, don't just throw the can away. **Save it!** But please avoid collecting any steel cans. You can't get anything for them. To pick out aluminium cans from steel ones, you can use a magnet. 5,000 cans earn £50. And £50 feeds a hungry African child for a long, long time!

CAN-AID

3. Objects: verb base + *ing* or infinitive? (1.1.3.1 and 1.1.3.2)

Larry has written a composition with the title 'My likes and dislikes'.

Complete it by giving the correct form of the words in brackets.

First, I am going to tell you about the things I like. I ([1] enjoy/play) **(= enjoy playing)** tennis and I ([2] be fond of/swim). Last year I ([3] succeed in/pass) my junior life-saver's test, and I ([4] hope/take) the senior test next year. I ([5] want/train) as a teacher of physical education when I leave school. If the weather is fine, I always ([6] like/be) out-of-doors, if possible, but I ([7] prefer/stay) indoors when it is cold or wet. However, it ([8] be fun/go) to a disco on a cold winter's evening, even though I ([9] not be good at/dance).

Now, some of the things I do not like. I ([10] start/smoke) when I was only 12, but I ([11] stop/buy) cigarettes three years ago, and I simply ([12] hate/smell) tobacco smoke now. I believe it ([13] be always best/tell) the truth, so I ([14] dislike/lie) and it makes me very angry when someone does something wrong and then ([15] deny/do) it.

4. Verbs with two objects (1.1.4)

David and Kate have made this list of presents to give their relations this Christmas.

Use it to complete the conversation they had while preparing it.

> Stella – get her a record of Vivaldi
> Mary and Bill – find a pair of matching suitcases
> Claire – buy a road atlas
> Louise and Marie – get some detective novels
> Aunt Flo – send some writing paper
> Helen – give a bicycle
> Charles – buy a new suit
> Andrew – give an electric shaver

David: What shall we give Stella?
Kate: She likes music. Wouldn't it be nice to
[1]____ **(= get her a record of Vivaldi?)**
David: Yes, that's fine. Mary and Bill travel a lot. I thought of [2]____.
Kate: Good idea. Now, Claire. She uses her car a lot. What about [3]____?
David: Excellent. Next, there's Louise and Marie.
Kate: They love reading. Let's [4]____.
David: OK. You choose them. Now, poor old Aunt Flo. She spends her time writing letters to everyone. It would make sense to [5]____.
Kate: Right. What about Helen?
David: I'm thinking of [6]____, because she has such a long walk to school each day.
Kate: She'll love it! Now, Charles. He needs to look smart now he's got this new job. I thought it would be a good idea to [7]____.
David: Yes, it would. And Andrew's growing a beard. How about [8]____?

5. Verbs with two objects (1.1.4)

Complete this story. Choose one of the verbs in the box for each gap, and put it into a suitable form.

say	tell	describe	explain	show	complain

The leader ¹___ (= **told**) the climbing party that they would all climb the mountain the next day. She ²___ that they would all have to set out at six o'clock in the morning. Then she began to ³___ the route to them. She hadn't ⁴___ them very much, when all the lights suddenly went out. An electrician came into the hut and ⁵___ the leader that the electricity supply had failed. He ⁶___ that he could not reconnect it before the next day. The leader ⁷___ this to the climbers. She ⁸___ that it meant they would have to wait until another day. Some of the climbers ⁹___ to her that they were very disappointed by this news. At this she got rather angry and said, 'Good climbers shouldn't ¹⁰___ their disappointment to each other like that. Don't you think I am disappointed too? But I try not to ¹¹___ it to anyone because, like a cold, disappointment is easily caught.'

6. Passive when cause is not known (1.1.7 and 1.1.9)

Jerry Keen came home soon after a crime had taken place in his house. He is telling the police what he saw.

Use the words under each picture to make sentences.

1. a window/break
   (= A window had been broken, but I've no idea who broke it.)

2. the radio/ turn on
3. the dog/tie up

4. the cupboards/ empty
5. the carpet/ roll up
6. the bath/fill

7. two bottles of beer/drink
8. a large cake/eat
9. my TV/steal

3

7. Passive when the agent is interesting (1.1.7)

Make sentences about the pictures.

1. pull/monkey   2. stop/policeman

3. chase/bull   4. steal/bird

5. strike/lightning   6. bite/snake

1. What happened to Andy's nose?
   (= It was pulled by a monkey!)
2. What happened to John?
3. What happened to the campers?
4. What happened to the ring?
5. What happened to the tree?
6. What happened to the little girl?

8. Passive with two objects (1.1.8)

Rewrite this news report, so that the object of each sentence becomes its subject, and the subject becomes its object.

A large sum of money was recently offered to Carlton Hospital. **(= Carlton Hospital was recently offered a large sum of money.)** News of this gift was sent to the Carlton Observer by the hospital chairman. The task of investigating the story was given to one of our youngest reporters.

Some years ago Mrs Peabody was given a new heart at Carlton Hospital. Afterwards the doctor who did the operation was promised a gift of money.

The money was handed to the hospital chairman yesterday, by Mrs Peabody's son.

9. Passive when there is no agent (1.1.7 and 1.1.9)

Look at the skeleton opposite, and complete these two verses of a famous Black American song.

The *foot* bone's connected to the *leg* bone,
The *leg* bone's connected to the _____ bone,
The _____ bone's connected to the _____ bone,
The _____ bone's connected to the _____ bone,
The _____ bone's connected to the _____ bone,
The _____ bone's connected to the _____ bone,
Oh, hear the word of the Lord!

The *head* bone's connected to the *neck* bone,
The *neck* bone's connected to the _____ bone,
The _____ bone's connected to the _____ bone,
The _____ bone's connected to the _____ bone,
The _____ bone's connected to the _____ bone,
The _____ bone's connected to the _____ bone,
Oh, hear the word of the Lord!

Write/Say/Sing the same verses again, using *join onto* or *attach to* instead of *connect to*.

Also do the song once in the plural.
Begin: 'Our foot bones are connected to our leg bones', etc.

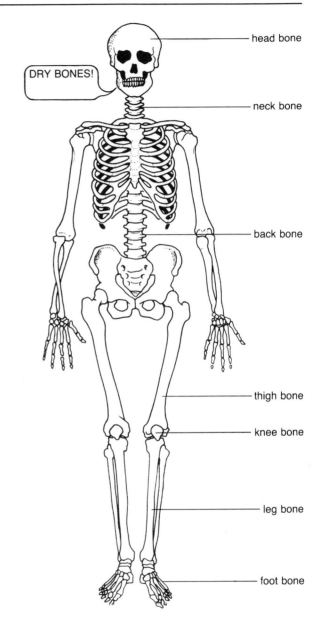

DRY BONES!

head bone
neck bone
back bone
thigh bone
knee bone
leg bone
foot bone

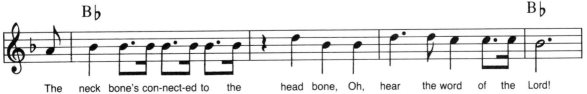

The neck bone's con-nect-ed to the head bone, Oh, hear the word of the Lord!

5

10. Passives in various tenses (1.1.7 to 1.1.9)

Below are descriptions of three different types of bicycle.

Complete each description by giving the correct passive form of the verb in brackets.

Woman's standard bicycle
When standard bicycles
(1 invent)
(= were invented)
in the late nineteenth century, long skirts
(2 wear) by most women riders, and so women's bicycles
(3 make) without crossbars ever since. Some makers still leave off the crossbar on women's bikes, even though long skirts (4 not use) by women cyclists nowadays. But standard bikes without crossbars are not as strong, so they
(5 should avoid) if you want to ride hard and fast.

Racing bicycle
Racing bikes are much more streamlined than standards and (6 sometimes build) specially to suit a particular rider. They are very light and (7 can carry) easily. Their tyres and wheels (8 design) for quick changes.

Small wheel bicycle
The small wheel bicycle is good in city traffic and (9 can fold up) so that it (10 can put) in the back of a car. The seat and handlebars (11 can adjust) to fit any size of rider. But the small wheels and high seats make riding hard work on long trips.

11. The passive with *get* (1.1.10)

This chart gives some important facts and figures about life in Seahampton last year.

1	Couples married	251
2	Couples divorced	73
3	People killed on the roads	36
4	People injured at work	384
5	People injured at home	414
6	Lost children	29
7	New houses built	189
8	Broken street lights	45
9	Stolen cars	111
10	Homes burgled	54

Write the questions for each number.
1. ___? 251.
   (= How many couples got married last year?)
2. ___? 73.
3. ___? 36.
4. ___? 384.
5. ___? 414.
6. ___? 29,
7. ___? 189.
8. ___? 45.
9. ___? 111.
10. ___? 54.

12. Adverbials of manner (1.1.11)

Read the adverbials in this box. Which of them are adverbials of manner?

angrily	on television
at ten o'clock	quickly
bravely	quietly
down by the riverside	upside down
in a very unusual way	very successfully
in the daytime	wearily
in the park	without any sign of pain

Now add to each sentence below all the adverbials of manner from the box which make good sense with it. Put each adverbial in a correct position in the sentence.

1. My favourite artist always signed her pictures.
   (= My favourite artist always signed her pictures *in a very unusual way/upside down*.)
2. Olga swims.
3. Mario spends his money.
4. You've put the books back on the shelf.
5. The bees were buzzing.
6. The rescue party climbed the mountain for the third time that day.
7. He hid his feelings of disappointment from his family.
8. The Indian walked over the pieces of broken glass.
9. Do you think you could shut all the windows?
10. These animals sleep.
11. Some of my old schoolfriends have got married.

7

13. Adverbials of time and place (1.1.11)

A typist got confused when typing something for a magazine. In each sentence she typed the adverbial of time where the adverbial of place should have been, and vice versa. Underline the adverbials and rewrite the story as it should have been.

Richard Garner was born into a working-class family <u>at Cosford School</u> and received an ordinary schooling <u>on 9th September 1968.</u> (= **Richard Garner was born into a working-class family on 9th September 1968 and received an ordinary schooling at Cosford School.**) Few other children lived after the war, because many children had moved away in his village. But his lonely life changed from the nearby city, when hundreds of holidaymakers arrived every summer. They stayed every afternoon, and Richard played with their children in hotels and holiday camps.

When the sons and daughters of the holidaymakers returned through the long months of autumn, winter and spring, Richard wrote letters to their homes. One of these penfriends replied at Buckingham Palace, inviting him to stay eventually. There Richard discovered that his penfriend actually lived then!

14. Adverbs of frequency (1.1.12)

An interviewer is finding out about people's habits. She has chosen you as one of the people to interview.

Complete your conversation with the interviewer. The commonest adverbs of frequency are given in the box.

always annually daily generally monthly never often rarely seldom sometimes usually weekly yearly

Interviewer:	How often do you have your hair cut?
You:	(= **I generally have it cut at the beginning of each term.**)
Interviewer:	And how often do you wash your hair?
You:	
Interviewer:	How do you dry your hair after washing it?
You:	
Interviewer:	Do you ever change the colour of your hair?
You:	
Interviewer:	Do you do your hair with a brush or a comb?
You:	
Interviewer:	Do you wash your face with soap?
You:	
Interviewer:	Do you ever bite your nails?
You:	
Interviewer:	Now, my last question. If you wear socks, do you wear ones made of nylon, wool, or cotton?
You:	
Interviewer:	Thank you for answering my questions.

15. Position of adverbials (1.1.11, 1.1.12, 1.1.13 and 1.1.15)

Two adverbials are given after each sentence below. Only one of them is suitable in the position where the gap occurs. Decide which it is, then write it (either Across or Down) on the crossword puzzle below.

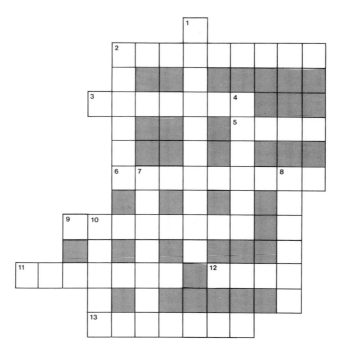

Across

2 The postman ____ came at eight o'clock. (yesterday/generally)

3 You may regret it if you buy a second-hand car ____. (hastily/usually)

5 I wouldn't ____ have guessed your name was Satako. (ever/here)

6 ____ I saw the doctor and she gave me some medicine. (Carefully/Yesterday)

9 Some plants flower only once and then die, so we have to plant new ones ____. (annually/scarcely)

11 My grandmother often fell asleep in her chair and fell to the ground ____. (usually/heavily)

12 He ____ turned the pages of his book. (idly/very)

13 She sat ____ on a high chair, offering everyone chocolates. (monthly/royally)

Down

1 I ____ saw Anton at the football ground. (everywhere/definitely)

2 I'll ____ rent my empty spare room to you. (gladly/weekly)

4 They saw each other ____ at a conference. (yearly/nearly)

7 In today's world, many men and women share the housework ____. (equally/usually)

8 We ____ watch television on Friday nights. (at home/always)

10 If you do the work as slowly as that, you will ____ finish it. (never/by ten)

16. *Yes/No* questions (1.2.1)

Some students are playing 'Twenty Questions' and trying to guess the object Jill has thought of. One of the rules of this game is that only *Yes/No* questions may be asked.

Continue the conversation like the examples.

Garcia:	Is the object a living thing?
Jill:	1 ____ (= **Yes, it is.**)
Toni:	Where does it live?
Jill:	2 ____ (= **I can't answer that. It isn't a *Yes/No* question.**)
Toni:	OK, then. Does it live on land?
Jill:	3 ____
Sophia:	Is it bigger than my hand?
Jill:	4 ____
Michel:	What does it eat?
Jill:	5 ____
Michel:	All right. Does it eat cooked food?
Jill:	6 ____
Garcia:	Can it fly?
Jill:	7 ____
Sophia:	Why can't it fly?
Jill:	8 ____
Toni:	Is it good at swimming?
Jill:	9 ____
Michel:	Is it a fish?
Jill:	10 ____

17. *Yes/No* questions (1.2.1)

Imagine you are carrying out a survey. Choose one of the topics from the box and write five *Yes/No* questions which would be useful in your survey.

Example (for what people eat):
Are you a big eater?
Do you take sugar in your tea?

But not:
How much do you eat for breakfast? (This question could not be answered with Yes or No.)

If you can, use your five questions on a friend.

Topics
What people eat.
How people spend their money.
How people work or study.
What people do in their free time.
How people get on with other members of the family (parents, brothers and sisters, etc.).

---

18. Declarative questions showing certainty (1.2.3)

A car owner has filled in his application for insurance. A clerk at the insurance company is now checking the answers. The car owner agrees with her each time, by answering either *Yes* or *No.*

Continue their conversation.

Examples:

1. **Clerk:**   **Your first name is Peter?**
   Car owner: **Yes, it is.**
2. **Clerk:**   **You haven't got a middle name?**
   Car owner: **No, I haven't.**

---

1. First name: Peter
2. Middle name: —
3. Surname: Small
4. Date of birth: 18 July 1960
5. Address: 12 Old Street, Kirby

6. Postcode: not known
7. Status:

   (please tick)

married	single	divorced
	✓	

8. Year you took the driving test: 1981
9. Are you insured by any other company? No
10. Date of last accident (if any): None
11. Occupation: Salesman
12. Employment status:

    (please tick)

employed	self-employed

unemployed	retired
✓	

13. Make of car: Dayton Ace
14. Size of engine: 1500 cc.
15. Year of manufacture: 1986
16. Registration number: C666RST

19. Positive tag questions showing uncertainty (1.2.4)

It is the First of April – April Fools' Day! The insurance clerk's boyfriend has filled in an application and posted it to her as a joke. The clerk cannot believe the answers, and is checking them over the phone – without realizing who she is talking to!

Continue the conversation.

Examples:

1. **Clerk:**   **Your name isn't really Jim John Jim George Zonk, is it?**
   Boyfriend: **Oh, yes, it is.**
   or:
1. **Clerk:**   **You don't really spell your surname Z-O-N-K, do you?**
   Boyfriend: **Oh, yes, I do.**

---

1. Name: Jim John Jim George ZONK
2. Date of birth: 29th February 1890
3. Address: Kirby Prison

4. Postcode: UR1 4ME
5. Status:

   for the tenth time

married	single	divorced
✓		

   (please tick)

6. Year you took the driving test: 1905
7. Date of last accident (if any): Yesterday
8. Occupation: Worm collector

20. Negative and positive tag questions (1.2.4)

Molly Hickson's small son Andy is looking at this picture. It's the first time he has seen Eskimos. He thinks he can understand how they live, but he is not quite sure.

Complete his conversation with his mother, by putting in the correct question tags. The first one has been done for you.

Andy: Eskimos live in very cold places, ^{1}____?
(= don't they)
Molly: Yes, they do. Near the North Pole, in fact.
Andy: They must wear a lot of clothes, then, ^{2}____?
Molly: Yes. They wear coats made of fur.
Andy: And their houses are made of snow, ^{3}____?

Molly: Yes. Look, this man here's making a house. They're called igloos, and they're actually very warm.
Andy: They can't buy things in shops, ^{4}____?
Molly: No, Andy, there are no shops near the North Pole! You know what they eat, ^{5}____?
Andy: Fish. This man's fishing through a hole in the ice, ^{6}____?
Molly: Yes, that's right. You can see what these men are doing too, ^{7}____?
Andy: They're mending a boat, ^{8}____?
Molly: Yes. It's called a kayak.
Andy: They have to use it when the ice melts, ^{9}____?
Molly: Yes. I expect the children like to go in the kayak.
Andy: But they don't go to school in it, ^{10}____ ?
Molly: No, there are no schools where they live.

21. Alternative questions (1.2.5)

Find in Box A something which answers each question, and in Box B something which is a sensible alternative to it. Then extend each question by adding an alternative question to it.

A	B
a magazine	tea
by bus	in your own car
your own family	on Friday
in hospital	potatoes
coffee	a friend's
rice	at home
tomorrow	a book

1. What will you read on the train?
   (= **Will you read a magazine or a book?**)
2. What will you have with your meat?
3. What will you drink with your meal?
4. When will you be leaving for Paris?
5. Who are you going to stay with in Scotland?
6. How do you travel to work in the mornings?
7. Where did you have your baby?

22. *Wh*-questions (1.2.6)

A journalist wrote these notes before an interview with Shirley Glebe, the actress.

1. Title of new film? 6. Studios?
2. Shirley's part in it? 7. Director?
3. Her co-star? 8. Date of release?
4. His part? 9. She'll earn?
5. Number of actors? 10. Cost of film?

After the interview she wrote this text.

NEW FILM ABOUT AGONY AUNT

The title of Shirley Glebe's new film is 'Dear Aunt Augusta'. In it she plays the part of an agony aunt. Her co-star in this film is Charles Burke. He plays her long-suffering husband. There are only five actors in the film altogether. The film is being made at Boreham Studios, and is directed by Nicholas Hamstein. It will be released in December. Shirley is being paid more than a million dollars. Altogether the film will cost about ten million.

Make the questions which the journalist actually asked Shirley Glebe during the interview.

Example:
1. *Notes* **Title of new film?**
   Article **The title of Shirley Glebe's new film is 'Dear Agony Aunt'.**
   (= *Question at interview* **'What is the title of your new film, Miss Glebe?' or: 'What is your new film called, Miss Glebe?'**)

23. Asking about subjects and objects (1.2.6)

There is going to be a dinner party. The hosts know that each guest has strong ideas about who he or she would like to sit next to. They have drawn a seating plan.

Make the questions and answers which the hosts say (two questions for each name on the plan).

Examples:
Who does Akiko want to sit next to? Antonio.
Who wants to sit next to Akiko? Ibrahim.

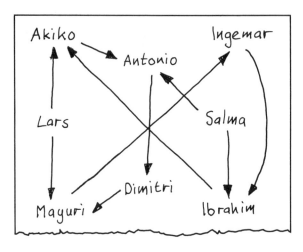

24. *What? Which? Who? When? Where? Why? How? How many?* (1.2.6)

Complete each of these questions with one of the *Wh-*question words above.

All the questions have silly answers. You can find these, in the same order, at the bottom of the page. Check whether you chose the correct *Wh-*word by comparing the question and answer.

1. ____ didn't the skeleton go to the dance?
2. ____ animal can jump higher than a tree?
3. ____ big men have been born in Cuba?
4. ____ do you know that a policeman is really strong?
5. ____ street in New York can everyone run down in exactly one minute?
6. ____ always thinks that two heads are better than one?
7. ____ do you find at the end of everything?
8. ____ do you usually find an elephant if you lose one?
9. ____ travels at the speed of sound, but doesn't have legs, wings or engines?
10. ____ is a car not a car?

25. Imperatives used to give instructions (1.3)

This is an instructions leaflet for a watch. To complete it, choose the right verb from the box to fill each gap. Use each verb once only. Use the appropriate form of the verb – positive imperative or negative imperative.

change	take out
drop	try
open	turn
position	wear
protect	wind
take	

CARE OF YOUR WATCH

¹___ (= **Take**) your watch to the makers for cleaning every two or three years. ²___ to clean it yourself. Always ³___ your watch against dust and heat. ⁴___ it when you are washing or swimming, and ⁵___ it onto any hard surface. ⁶___ the watch – it is automatic!

CHANGING BATTERIES

If your watch stops, ⁷___ the batteries. ⁸___ the back of the watch and ⁹___ the old batteries. Always ¹⁰___ the new batteries correctly (+ to +, – to –).

SETTING THE WATCH

Always ¹¹___ the hands of the watch in the clockwise direction.

26. Imperatives used to forbid something (1.3)

All these signs mean something is not allowed. Give their meaning. You will find the words in the box useful in your answers.

exceed	iron	park	pass
ride	smoke	sound your horn	turn

1. (= **Do not turn right here.**)

2.   3.

50

4.   5.   6.

7.   8.   9.

27. Negative statements (1.4.1 and 1.4.2)

Add a sensible negative clause to each sentence.

1. You can see through a window. (a wall)
   (= **You can see through a window, but you can't see through a wall.**)
2. You can ride through snow on a bicycle. (ice)
3. Small babies can drink from bottles. (cups)
4. Drivers may park where they see a Parking sign. (No Parking sign)
5. Some plants will grow well in a warm building. (out-of-doors)
6. Two hundred years ago people could travel by land and water. (air)
7. You can drink fresh water. (seawater)
8. In the seventeenth century people used to heat their homes with wood or coal. (electricity or gas)
9. You should eat a lot when you have a cold. (a fever)
10. Children ought to be put to bed if they look tired. (lively)

28. Negative questions (1.4.4)

Underline all the negative questions in this conversation.

Mary: Would you like a cigarette, Liz?
Liz: No, thanks.
Mary: Don't you smoke?
Liz: No.
Mary: Haven't you ever smoked?
Liz: No. Smoking's too expensive. And bad for your health.
Mary: You think I don't know that?
Liz: Can't you give it up?
Mary: I don't know how to. Do you?
Liz: Didn't you ever ask your doctor to help?
Mary: No. How could I? Would you like to talk to your doctor about something like that?
Liz: Isn't your doctor a very good listener, then?
Mary: I'm not sure.
Liz: Don't you know?
Mary: Mmm, well, no . . .
Liz: You haven't been to see him recently, have you?
Mary: No. Well, at least, not for three years.
Liz: Three years? Isn't it about time you did?
Mary: Perhaps.

29. Positive and negative questions with *Why?* (1.2.6 and 1.4.4)

A journalist is finding out how foreign visitors spend holidays in her country. She has a list of facts, which she turns into questions when she talks to a foreign visitor.

Here are the facts. Make the questions she asks.

1. Most people return to the same place year after year.
   (= Why do you return to the same place year after year?)
2. They don't like to come in any months except July and August.
   (= Why don't you like to come in any months except July and August?)
3. They won't eat our national food.
4. They prefer large hotels to small ones.
5. They don't bring their children with them.
6. They never go out alone.
7. They don't buy many presents to take home.
8. They usually arrive on a daytime flight.
9. They spend all their time on the beach.
10. They don't often hire a car.

30. *A lot, already, some, still, too, yet* (in positive statements); *any, much, either, neither, nor, yet* (in negative statements and questions) (1.4.3 and 1.4.5)

In this crossword puzzle, each clue is a sentence with one word missing. The correct word to fill each gap is one of those above.

Find the correct word and write it next to the same number in the puzzle (Across or Down, as appropriate).

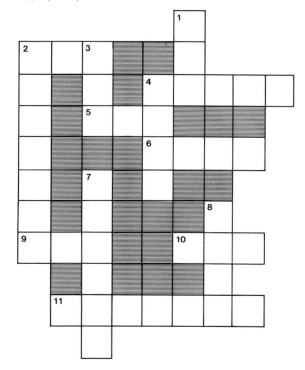

Across (Conversation A)

2. Have you got ____ apples?
4. Yes, we ____ have a few.
5. I'd like a kilo of oranges, ____.
6. Where shall I put them? You don't seem to have ____ room in your bag.
9. That's a nuisance, as I haven't finished shopping ____.
10. I'm afraid I can't help you, and ____ can the shop next door. We've both run out of paper bags.
11. And the supermarket hasn't got any, and ____ has the butcher!

Down (Conversation B)

1. There are a ____ of apples on your trees, aren't there?
2. Yes, and we've ____ picked about 200 kilos!
3. Are the pears ready ____?
4. Yes, I've got ____ nice soft ones indoors.
7. Soft ones? I don't like those. And I don't like very hard ones, ____.
8. I'll try to find ____ nice ones for you later.

31. Short responses (1.4.7)

Answer each statement with a short response beginning with *So*.

1. This exercise is about 'short responses'.
   (= So it is!)
2. We're on page 18.
3. We can do this exercise orally or in writing.
4. This is question number 4.
5. We've got six more questions to do after this one.
6. We'll be doing number 7 next.
7. This exercise refers to section 1.4.7 of *Active Grammar*.
8. We're doing this exercise very quickly.
9. We may be getting everything right, too.
10. All our answers to this exercise have begun with 'So'.
11. We should have learnt a lot by doing this exercise.

32. *So, too, also; neither, nor, either* (1.4.7)

Write sentences about life in your own country compared with life in England.

1. Most people in England want to own their own house.
   (= So do most people in my country/in Portugal.)
   (or = Oh, do they? People in my country don't.)
2. Most people in England don't work on Saturdays or Sundays.
   (= Neither do most people in my country/in Mexico.)
   (or = Oh, don't they? People in my country do.)
3. Most people in England get married before they are thirty.
4. Everyone in England stays at school until at least the age of 16.
5. Most people in England don't go to university.
6. Lots of people in England spend two or three hours each day watching television.
7. Most people in England can't understand nuclear physics.
8. Most people in England couldn't mend a computer, if they had to.
9. Most workers in England have four weeks' holiday every year.
10. Most people in England can't speak even one foreign language well.

33. *So, too, also* (1.4.7)

Choose one of the words or phrases in each set of brackets and use it to answer each statement.

1. London is in England. (Manchester, Berlin, Paris)
   (= So is Manchester.
   or = Manchester is also in England.
   or = Manchester is in England, too.)
2. Potatoes grow in the ground. (apples, oranges, onions)
3. Ducks can fly. (ostriches, penguins, swans)
4. Venus is one of the planets in the solar system. (Shakespeare, Mars, Mozart)
5. Britain has a royal family. (America, Japan, Brazil)
6. Christmas is one of the most important Christian festivals. (Easter, May Day, the Queen's Birthday)
7. Bach was a German composer. (Beethoven, Chopin, Tchaikovsky)
8. The year 1996 will have a February 29th. (the years 1997 and 1998, the year 1999, the year 2000)
9. Saudi Arabia is one of the world's big oil producers. (Belgium, Mexico, Switzerland)
10. Cricket is a national sport in Britain. (skiing and ice hockey, volleyball and basketball, football and rugby)
11. The Chinese had a writing system four thousand years ago. (the British, the Egyptians, the Russians)

34. Positive and negative opinions (1.4.8)

Complete this conversation twice. The first time, imagine that Alex is an *optimist*. The second time, imagine he is a *pessimist*. When two different verbs are given in the brackets, choose the better one.

Bill: The club tennis championships are tomorrow. Will you get into the finals this year?
Alex: 1. (expect) **(Optimist = I expect so.)**
                    (Pessimist = I don't expect so.
                    or   = I expect not.)
Bill: Have you had enough practice?
Alex: 2. (think)
Bill: Is the weather going to keep fine?
Alex: 3. (hope/be afraid)
Bill: There'll be the usual wonderful prizes for the winners, won't there?
Alex: 4. (suppose)
Bill: But you'll be feeling very tired by the end of the day, won't you?
Alex: 5. (hope/imagine)

35. Exclamations with *What . . . !* and *How . . . !* (1.5)

Tina Forthright is a politician who believes that people like strong speeches. She has written down some ideas and asked her secretary to change them into exclamations.

Read the ideas and continue the speech.

1. I am happy to talk to you today.
    (= **How happy I am to talk to you today!**)
2. It was a wonderful idea to give me the chance of talking to you on television.
    (= **What a wonderful idea it was to give me the chance of talking to you on television!**)
3. I am pleased that so many of you voted for me last week.
4. It was a pity that any of you voted for the other party.
5. The last government made terrible mistakes.
6. We have all become poor in the last ten years.
7. There are a lot of problems for me to solve.
8. I shall have to be very clever to find answers to all of them.
9. There were a lot of useless strikes last winter.
10. We must all work hard in future.
11. There will be a wonderful time in front of us, if you all do as I tell you.

Section two:

The complex sentence

36. Connecting with *and* or *but* (2.1 and 2.2)

Various people have pulled pieces of paper out of a 'lucky dip' to find out about their fortunes in the future.

Complete the meaning of each of them by adding *and* or *but*.

1. Monday will be a difficult day for you ____ Tuesday and Wednesday will be better.
2. This year you will have a chance to learn a new language ____ you will go to the country where it is spoken.
3. In a year or two from now you will marry ____ you will have several children.
4. This year you will be bored with your job ____ next year you will have more interesting work to do.
5. You are about to lose one of your best friends ____ you will soon make another.
6. You will start to keep a diary ____ one day you will use it to write a novel about your life.
7. This winter your health won't be very good ____ you will spend several weeks in bed.
8. Next weekend is a good time to visit friends ____ the weekend afterwards you should stay at home.
9. You are going to enter a competition soon ____ you won't win a prize.
10. The coming year will be a very expensive one ____ you will need to borrow money from the bank.

37. *Who* and *which* as subjects of restrictive relative clauses (2.3.1)

Below are the titles and descriptions of some imaginary films, as they appear on the theatre page of a London newspaper.

Combine the titles and descriptions into complex sentences.

1. 'Farmer and Father' – a man gives his farm to his three daughters.
   (= 'Farmer and Father' is (a film) about a man who gives his farm to his three daughters.)
2. 'The Storm' – a ship is blown onto a desert island.
   (= 'The Storm' is (a film) about a ship which is blown onto a desert island.)
3. 'Doctor Poison' – a doctor kills his three wives because he finds out none of them has any money.
4. 'Go home, Romeo!' – a family hate their daughter's boyfriend.
5. 'Quake Port' – an airport is hit by an earthquake.
6. 'Growing Rich' – a tree has flowers made of pure gold.
7. 'Star Politics' – a Martian woman pretends to be the Prime Minister.
8. 'Lost at Sea' – a fishing boat is sunk by angry whales.
9. 'No Points East' – cowboys stop the building of a railway across their land.
10. 'The Cat and I' – a cat with one eye can read its owner's thoughts.
11. 'Cliff Hanger' – a seaside hotel falls into the sea.
12. 'Lost World' – a plane crash in the mountains leads to the discovery of a lost civilization.

38. Using relative clauses to state preferences (2.3.1)

Think about the kinds of people and things you like. The list of topics in the box is there to help you, but you can choose other topics, if you wish.

Make sentences about 6 of your preferences.

Examples:
I prefer music which is modern and good for dancing.
I prefer teachers who speak quietly and look smart.

music	films	scenery
teachers	food	work
books	poems	friends
stories	children	clothes
TV shows	politicians	art

39. *Whose* in relative clauses (2.3.1)

Imagine you are at the party which you can see in the picture below. You are askig your host who everybody is.

Complete the conversation by adding appropriate relative clauses, made up of the matching words from A and B.

	A	B
1.	hands	against the mirror
2.	back	on the cat
3.	beard	on the door-handle
4.	foot	against the wall
5.	glasses	on the back of the chair
6.	hand	on Carol Pine's knee
7.	head	on top of her head
8.	nose	in the cream

Host: You know everybody here, don't you?
You: No. In fact, I don't know anybody at all, really. What's the name of that man <u>1</u>___?
(= **whose hands are on the back of the chair**)
Host: That's Tom Scott.
You: And that girl <u>2</u>___ ?
Host: Jill Penny. She's nice.
You: Is she? And who's that man <u>3</u>___ ?
Host: Oh, he's John Bruce. He's clumsy, isn't he?
You: Can you tell me about the girl <u>4</u>___ ?
Host: You must be looking at Carol Pine. She loves animals, really.
You: I'd never have guessed. What does that very beautiful girl <u>5</u>___ call herself?
Host: She's Mary Oaks. Actually, she wears an awful lot of make-up.
You: Well, it suits her. What's the name of the man <u>6</u>___ ?
Host: You mean Jack Fisher. He works in a bank.
You: Does he really? Who's that sloppy man <u>7</u>___ ?
Host: Roger Sneed? He's really in love with Carol, you know!
You: There's one more whose name I don't know. It's the girl <u>8</u>___.
Host: That's Vera Plum. You'd like her. Come on, I'll introduce you.

40. Non-restrictive relative clauses (2.3.1)

Here are some pictures of national emblems from a number of countries.
Write about each emblem twice.

1. England/rose/
   pink flower

(England) One of the emblems of England is the rose, which is a pink flower.
(rose) The rose, which is one of the emblems of England, is a pink flower.

2. Scotland/thistle/
   plant with sharp
   prickles

3. Ireland/shamrock/
   lucky kind of leaf

4. Wales/daffodil/
   yellow spring flower

5. New Zealand/kiwi/
   bird that can't fly

6. Australia/koala
   bear/tree-loving
   animal

7. America/eagle/
   bird of the mountains

8. Nepal/kris/long
   kind of knife

41. Leaving relative pronoun *that* out of restrictive relative clauses after superlatives (2.3.1)

The travel agents of Superbia want us to believe that everything there is the best in the world.
   Write sentences for their advertisements using the notes below.

In Superbia you can

1. climb high mountains
   (= We have the highest mountains you will ever climb!)
2. fish in good rivers
3. lie and play on sunny beaches
4. wander in large forests
5. swim in warm seas
6. eat fine food
7. stay at luxurious hotels
8. photograph beautiful views
9. talk to friendly people
10. watch wildlife in wonderful parks
11. buy unusual souvenirs

42. Non-restrictive relative clauses with prepositions (2.3.1)

A detective is investigating a theft which happened during a birthday party. For his official report, he is combining the information given by different people. Continue his report.

1. The party took place in the dining room.

   The Welsbys' bedroom is above it.

   (= The party took place in the dining room, above which is the Welsbys' bedroom.)

2. Under their bed there is a strong-box.

   Mrs Welsby kept all her jewelry in it.

3. There were six guests.

   Mrs Welsby had received a present from each of them.

4. Mr Welsby noticed that Mr Lee smelled strongly of after-shave lotion.

   He was talking to him about golf.

5. Mr Hardy asked Mr Welsby where he could wash his hands.

   He had been stroking the Welsbys' dog with them.

6. Mr Welsby told Mr Hardy to follow Mr Lee.

   He had just been asked a similar question by him.

7. Suddenly all the lights went out in the dining room.

   The guests were starting to eat supper in it.

8. The clock struck nine while the lights were out.

   Mrs Welsby was standing close to it.

9. Mrs Welsby ran upstairs to her bedroom.

   There was a strong smell of after-shave in it.

10. She opened her strong-box.

    All her jewelry had been taken from it.

43. *That* as subject, or left out as object, in restrictive relative clauses (2.3.1.1)

In each of the following sentences, write the word *that* only if it is grammatically necessary.

1. The pen _____ I borrowed from my friend soon ran out of ink.
2. The pen _____ cost me £3 quickly ran out of ink.
3. The hotel _____ opened in South Street five years ago has now closed.
4. The hotel _____ we stayed at last year has now closed.
5. The books _____ we read for school examinations weren't always very interesting.
6. I'd like one of those Walkman transistors _____ you can listen to on the bus without anyone else hearing.
7. For Christmas I'd like a home computer _____ has a large memory.
8. I also need a new watch to replace the one _____ Aunt Louise gave me for my birthday.
9. 'Gandhi' is an example of a serious film _____ has won an Oscar.
10. When did you last eat one of those beautiful tasty apples _____ are supposed to keep the doctor away?

44. Using *with*/*without* instead of relative clauses (2.3.1.1 and 2.3.6)

Imagine you are a travel agent who has been asked for advice about hotels in a seaside town. Refer to the information chart and make ten sentences from the table below it.

Example:
If you don't mind a room without a bath, you could stay at the Liberty.

Name of Hotel	Number of Rooms	Facilities
Grand	460	
Ritz	200	
Carlton	84	
Liberty	12	

Key: Bath in every room   TV in every room   Telephone in every room

Restaurant [R]   Swimming pool   Central heating

All rooms have a view of the sea   Own bus service

If you	want require must have don't mind 'd be content with	a room a hotel	with without	lots of people in it, not many people in it, a view of the sea, a bath, a television, a restaurant, a telephone, a swimming pool, central heating, its own bus service,	you could	book in at . . . stay at . . . try . . . put up at . . .

45. Reduced relative clauses (2.3.1.1)

Astronaut Glenn Chambers is showing his family some photographs that were taken on his recent voyage to the moon.

Look at the photos and think of the words Glenn says. He uses relative clauses without a relative pronoun.

5. Glenn fell into a hole.

6. Glenn brought back a moon rock.

1. The astronauts all had a wonderful view of Earth.
   (= **'That's the wonderful view of Earth we all had.'**)

2. Glenn took a photo when everybody was weightless.
   (= **'That's the photo I took when everybody was weightless.'**)

7. The landing party travelled in a moon-buggy.

8. Oliver and Glenn played football with a tin box.

3. Glenn lost a tool during his spacewalk.

4. The astronauts had to eat their food from plastic bags.

9. Oliver and Glenn raised a flag on the moon.

10. The astronauts saw parachutists coming to rescue them.

46. Participle constructions instead of relative clauses (2.3.1.1)

At the Wetherton Sports Club the secretary has written a notice. She decides to shorten it in the ways shown in the examples. Continue.

1. Members *who use* (= **using)** the swimming pool are asked to observe the following rules *which have been decided on* (= **decided on)** by your committee:
2. Keys which are taken from the lockers should be worn round swimmers' wrists using the bands which are provided.
3. Towels which are borrowed from the club should be placed after use in the baskets which stand near the entrances.
4. Children who swim in either the small or the large pool must be in the care of their parents or other adults who are qualified to look after them.
5. Members who enter the deep end of the large pool must be strong swimmers.
6. Swimmers who dive from the high board should always make sure no swimmers are underneath them.
7. Food which is purchased in the snack bar must not be eaten at the poolside.
8. Members who break any of these rules will be fined.

47. Mixed types of relative clauses (2.3.1)

Complete the following extract from a short story by choosing the word in the brackets which is correct.
(– means that no relative pronoun is suggested.)

'People ([1] who/ –) (= **who)** live in glass houses shouldn't throw stones,' said Miss Fothergay, ([2] that/ who) was feeling rather hurt by Jocelyn's remarks. 'You know ([3] whom/ –) I'm talking about, don't you?' she went on.

Jocelyn himself, ([4] whose/that) remarks had not been intended to hurt anyone, simply looked puzzled by Miss Fothergay's anger, and began nervously to finger the pile of buns ([5] which/ –) lying in the centre of the table, and didn't reply. Miss Fothergay looked accusingly at the bun ([6] that/who) Jocelyn already had on his plate, and Jocelyn, ([7] that/who) hated to be thought greedy, quickly drew back his hand from the pile of buns, ([8] which/ –) caused him to knock over his cup of tea. He looked round desperately for something with ([9] that/which) to dry it up.

'Haven't you got anything ([10] that/whom) I can clean up this mess with?' he asked quietly.

'Isn't that a handkerchief ([11] who/that) I can see in your pocket?' Miss Fothergay asked sarcastically.

'Only one ([12] whose/ –) you gave me for Christmas,' Jocelyn replied.

'Why don't you use it, then?' Miss Fothergay continued. 'My feelings are surely the last thing ([13] that/ –) to be considered in an emergency like this.'

48. *What* as subject of noun clause (2.3.2)

The people in the pictures below have all seen, heard or felt something unusual.

Write about each of them using the words given. Begin each sentence with *What . . .*

1. Caroline was surprised. She said,

    'Just look at the height of that tree!'

    (= **What surprised Caroline was the height of the tree.**)

2. John was interested. He said,

    'Have you seen the size of the shark's teeth?'

3. Peter was scared. He said,

    'Can you see the length of the snake?'

4. Alice was horrified. She said,

    'Just listen to the roar of the lions!'

5. The visitor was amazed. He said,

    'Just look at the number of stars in the sky!'

6. Helen was worried. She said,

    'Have you felt the weight of the bags?'

7. The commentator was excited. He said,

    'Just look at the strength of Superyouth's arms!'

8. Sharon was amused. She said,

    'I've never seen anything so funny as the sight of Jill riding a camel!'

49. *What* as object of noun clause (2.3.2)

Complete each of the following so that it is a true statement about yourself.

1. What I like to eat most is . . .
2. What I'm rather afraid of doing is . . .
3. What I like to do best at the weekends is . . .
4. What I hate to have to talk about is . . .
5. What I've seen in pictures, and would like to see with my own eyes, is . . .

50. Adverbial clauses of time (2.3.3)

A bird-lover has been watching some birds (swallows) which travel from Africa to Europe every spring.
   Complete her diary by putting a word or phrase from the box in each gap.

after   as soon as   since   till

This year the swallows did not arrive ¹___ 2nd June. ²___ they got here they started building their nests. ³___ the eggs are laid, one bird is always in the nest. The other flies backwards and forwards to get food for the family. ⁴___ it has brought back one mouthful, it flies off for more, without wasting any time at the nest.
   The swallows will be here ⁵___ the end of September. ⁶___ that they will fly off to Africa, and it will be another six or seven months ⁷___ I see them again. I have been watching swallows every year ⁸___ I came to live in this village. That was four years ago. I wonder if it is the same birds which have been coming back ⁹___ the first year I was here? ¹⁰___ seeing them return to my house year after year, I feel as if they were old friends of the family.

51. Tenses in time clauses (2.3.3)

The police want to catch a gang of criminals. The notes below are the policemen's plan. Make them into full sentences. Put the verbs into the correct tenses (present simple, present progressive or future simple) and put *when* or *while* in the correct place in each sentence.

1. the gang buy the drugs – our agents tell us
   (= **When the gang buy the drugs, our agents will tell us.**)
2. we do nothing – they cross the sea in their boat
   (= **We will do nothing while they are crossing the sea in their boat.**)
3. we stay out of sight – they land on our coast
4. we take the number of their van – they load the drugs into it
5. the van drives off – some of us arrest the crew of the boat
6. the van drives inland – the rest of us follow it in an unmarked car
7. the gang reach their destination – they hand over the drugs to their customers
8. the gang stay and watch – the customers check the quality of the goods
9. the gang and customers are busy with each other – we move in and catch them all red-handed
10. we take our prisoners to the nearest police station – we radio news of our success to headquarters in London

52. Clauses of reason and purpose (2.3.3)

On his Australian television show 'Talking to Wayne', Wayne Yallop interviews famous people from all over the world. Here is one of his interviews. Read it and then do the exercise.

Wayne: My guest this evening is Mary Culpepper, the famous singer. Welcome to my show, Mary. Nice of you to agree to appear on it.

Mary: I've always wanted to meet you, Wayne.

Wayne: Is that so? Now you came to Australia a year ago, Mary. Why did you come?

Mary: I couldn't stand the weâther in England any longer.

Wayne: Is that right? But why Australia? Had you some special purpose in coming here?

Mary: Yes, I've always dreamed of singing at the famous Sydney Opera.

Wayne: But you have never sung there, have you? How do you explain that?

Mary: I've had a sore throat all summer.

Wayne: I hear you'll soon be going to New York. What for?

Mary: To have an operation on my throat.

Wayne: Will you be coming back here afterwards?

Mary: No, I'll be staying in the States.

Wayne: Why's that, Mary?

Mary: I want to spend more time with my husband, who's working there.

Wayne: Why doesn't he come and work here in Australia too?

Mary: He's just gone into American politics. He wants to be President!

By choosing the words from the boxes which fit together, make two different accounts of the interview opposite.

Mary Culpepper, the famous singer, agreed to		
appear on the 'Talking to Wayne' show	because so that	
she could meet she likes	Wayne Yallop.	
She came to Australia a year ago	as so as to	
escape the English weather. English weather is so awful.	She had hoped	
to sing at the Sydney Opera,	because so that	
she could fulfil a dream, it is so famous,	but in fact she has never	
done so,	as so as to	rest her voice. her voice still needs rest.
Soon Mary will be leaving for America	because so that	
she can have she needs	an operation on her bad throat.	
Then she plans to remain in the States	as so that	
her husband is working there. she can see more of her husband.	It seems that	
Mr Culpepper wants to remain in the States,		
since so that	he can try to become President. he has gone into American politics.	

53. **Adverbial clauses of result (2.3.3)**

Finish each sentence about a pair of pictures by adding *(and) so* or *and therefore*, with a suitable clause.

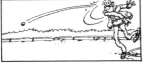

1. The dog was barking at the cat . . .
   (= The dog was barking at the cat, (and) so/and therefore Jim threw a stone at it.)

2. As soon as Helga left the house it started to rain, . . .

3. Arthur was feeling very hungry, . . .

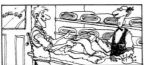

4. Richard's new trousers were too long for him, . . .

5. Ingrid's car was terribly dirty, . . .

6. Max's wife was feeling unhappy, . . .

54. *So* + Adj/Adv + *that,* showing result (2.3.3)

Finish these sentences about the same pictures, like the new example.

1. The dog was barking at the cat so loudly . . .
   (= The dog was barking at the cat so loudly that Jim threw a stone at it.)
2. The rain began to come down so hard . . .
3. Arthur suddenly felt so hungry . . .
4. Richard's new trousers were so long . . .
5. Ingrid was so ashamed of her dirty car . . .
6. Max was so sorry for his wife . . .

55. *So* and *therefore* expressing results or logical conclusions (2.3.3)

This exercise is about *syllogisms*. There are three statements in a syllogism, and the third must be a logical conclusion or result of the first two.

Example:
All human beings have a mother.
Napoleon was a human being.
So/Therefore Napoleon had a mother.

There are also false syllogisms, that is, ones in which the third statement is *not* a logical conclusion or result of the first two.

Example:
Cats like milk.
My sister likes milk, too.
So/Therefore my sister is a cat.

Read the following syllogisms and decide whether they are true or false.

1. Heathrow is the busiest airport in the world.
   TWA flies to all the world's busy airports.
   So TWA flies to Heathrow.
2. All insects have six legs.
   The spider has eight legs.
   Therefore the spider is not an insect.
3. Meat-eating animals often catch their food at night.
   My brother likes eating meat.
   So my brother often catches his food at night.
4. The Japanese and the British love gardens.
   Japan and Britain are islands.
   So people who love gardens always live on islands.
5. Children lose things if they are careless.
   Children start to lose their first teeth when they are 5 years old.
   So five-year-old children lose their teeth because they are careless.
6. Roses smell sweet.
   My mother loves all sweet-smelling flowers.
   So my mother likes roses.
7. One of the things blackbirds eat is worms.
   Worms come out of the ground when it rains.
   So blackbirds eat only when it rains.

56. *So* + Adj/Adv + *that*; *such* + N + *that*, showing result (2.3.3)

There are parking problems in the city of Berry. The chairman of the Roads Committee is writing a report to the city council. Complete it from his notes.

1. Banks open for a very short time – there are always crowds of customers.
   (= Banks open for such a short time that there are always crowds of customers.)
2. Our buses are very large – no cars can park along bus routes.
   (= Our buses are so large that no cars can park along bus routes.)
3. Car parks are very far from the town centre – shoppers won't use them.
4. Many streets are very narrow – cars can park on one side only.
5. Traffic wardens work very slowly – most drivers who break the rules aren't caught.
6. Parking meters break down very easily – parking spaces are often out of use.
7. Traffic wardens receive a very small salary – we can't find enough of them.
8. Some drivers know the wardens' habits very well – they move their cars before they're caught.
9. Some drivers have a very great deal of money – they drive larger cars than they really need.
10. Offenders have to pay very small fines – they simply laugh at them.

57. *So that* + clause, as a suggestion for improving things (2.3.3)

Think of ways of solving the problems mentioned in the chairman's report. (See Exercise 56.) Make suggestions for improvements.

Examples:
The banks should open for a longer time, so that there aren't always crowds of customers.
Buses should be smaller, so that cars can park along bus routes.

58. *So that* + clause of purpose; *so* + Adj/Adv + *that* + clause of result (2.3.3)

Complete as many as possible of the following sentences, so that they are true statements about yourself. Where alternatives are given (e.g. quickly/carefully) use the word you prefer.

1. I usually do my work as quickly/carefully as possible so that . . .
2. I usually work so fast/slowly that . . .
3. I think English is so interesting/boring that . . .
4. I am learning English so that . . .
5. In everything I do I am usually so lucky/unlucky that . . .
6. I always eat just enough/as little as possible/as much as possible/so that . . .
7. I eat so little/much that . . .

59. Adverbial clauses of contrast (2.3.3)

Martin Leatherskin is completely anti-social, as these pictures show.

Look at each picture and then make a sentence from the table. Note that you must also choose the correct position of *though* or *although* (either at the beginning, or in the middle, depending on the sense).

(Although) (Though)	photography was forbidden in the gallery, he stood on the wrong side of the escalator, the light warned him not to cross, a very old person was standing right in front of him, he lit up a cigarette, he got out and left his car,	(although) (though)	he would not give up his seat. he was in a no-smoking compartment. he took lots of pictures. he was in a no-parking area. someone wanted to pass. he marched across the road.

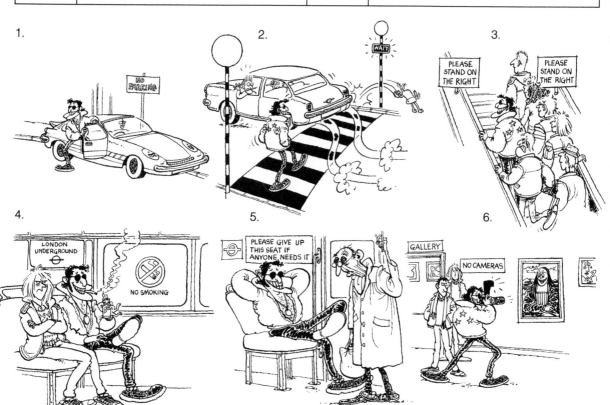

1.

2.

3.

4.

5.

6.

60. Clauses of comparison (2.3.4)

A large egg weighs 60 grammes and contains 90 calories of energy. An average apple weighs 140 grammes (= more), but has only 60 calories (= less) than an egg.

Read this table and make comparisons.

Examples:
An egg weighs less than an apple. But it contains more energy/calories.
An apple weighs more than an egg. But it contains less energy/fewer calories.
An egg and a slice of brown bread weigh the same. But an egg has more energy in it.

	Weight	Calories
Egg	60 g	90
Apple	140 g	60
Orange	220 g	70
Potato	200 g	200
Banana	200 g	80
Small bar of chocolate	120 g	580
Slice of brown bread	60 g	55

61. Clauses of comparison (2.3.4)

You have given the police a description of a man and a woman whom they want to interview. Now they are showing you photographs for comparison. What might you say?

Examples:
No, the woman's hair was fairer than that.
Her eyes were bigger than those in the photograph.

face (thin/fat)
hair (dark/fair/short/long/straight/curly)
eyes (big/small/round/narrow/close together)
nose (thin/wide/long/short)
teeth (good/bad)
mouth (big/small)

Police photograph of man

The man you remember seeing

fringe (long/short)
eyebrows (thin/bushy)
ears (big/small)
lips (thin/thick)
chin (pointed/rounded/square)

Police photograph of woman

The woman you remember seeing

62. Mixed links: *and, but, or;* relative pronouns; conjunctions with adverbial clauses (2.1–2.3.4)

Here is an extract from 'Just a Holiday Romance' by Rosa Lovejoy. Complete the extract, choosing from the words below. (Note that you will need to use some of them more than once.)

after	although	and	as	because	but
how	or	since	so	so that	until	when
whereas	while	who	whom		

¹____ Tina came into the breakfast room she chose a seat opposite the door ²____ she could observe the other guests ³____ they entered. ⁴____ she would never have admitted it, there was one guest ⁵____ particularly interested her – the tall man with dark hair ⁶____ she had met the previous night, ⁷____ they were going through the customs at Costa Dorada airport. Most of the passengers had looked tired and uncomfortable, ⁸____ he looked cool and relaxed. He had stood just beside her, ⁹____ thinking that she needed help with her suitcase he had offered to carry it to the waiting bus. She had declined his offer, ¹⁰____ she had never liked playing the part of the helpless female, ¹¹____ she knew she could manage the suitcase herself. He had only smiled in an understanding way, as if he understood exactly ¹²____ she felt. Yet his smile seemed to say, 'You can accept my offer ¹³____ refuse it, ¹⁴____ sooner or later we'll get to know each other.' Then, ¹⁵____ they had arrived at the hotel there was a long delay ¹⁶____ the clerk had filled in the wrong dates for their group. They had to wait ¹⁷____ the manager came to sort things out, ¹⁸____ by this time Tina was really tired. ¹⁹____ she had been unwilling to accept help from the man before, this time she did not protest ²⁰____, without waiting for a porter, he picked up her case and carried it to the lift.

63. Conditional clauses: position of *if* (2.3.6)

This is a leaflet from the Friends of the Countryside. In each line, the word *if* is missing once – either at the beginning, or in the middle.

Write each sentence out again with *if* in the right place.

1	____you leave plastic bags in fields	____ animals may eat them.
2	____an animal eats a plastic bag	____ it can kill it.
3	____you throw a broken bottle away	____ someone may cut his foot on it.
4	____a piece of glass may cause a fire	____ the sun shines on it.
5	____cows and sheep often get lost	____ gates are left open.
6	____dogs get into a field with sheep	____ lambs may be born dead.
7	____you pick wild flowers	____ they may never grow again.
8	____you may break the law	____ you collect birds' eggs.
9	____fires may start	____ cigarettes are thrown into dry grass.

64. Conditional clauses: hypothetical conditions (2.3.6)

Sara is day-dreaming about things which could never really happen. Read her thoughts, and then invent a conclusion to each idea.

1. Let's imagine I'm a frog, and my teacher is a fly!
   (= If I were a frog and my teacher was a fly, I'd eat him!)
2. How's this for an idea – the sun is an orange and I've got wings!
3. I know – I'm the richest woman in the world and the people of Africa are still starving.
4. Let's imagine I have one blue eye and one brown one.
5. Now I'm going to imagine I have wheels on the ends of my legs instead of feet.
6. Here's an interesting thought – I'm a girl for six months of each year and a boy for the other six!

65. Conditional clauses: real possibilities (2.3.6)

The following are well-known scientific facts or natural laws. Put the verbs into suitable tenses.

1. If the temperature of water (drop) to freezing point, it (turn) into ice.
   (= If the temperature of water drops to freezing point, it turns into ice.)
2. If water (reach) boiling point, it (change) into steam.
3. If we (add) oil and water together, the oil (float) on top.
4. If you (throw) a stone into the air, gravity (pull) it back to earth again.
5. If an iron object (stand) in the open air for long, it (become) rusty.
6. If we (leave) silver in the sunlight, it (go) black.
7. If a cloud (release) electricity, this (find) the shortest way to the ground.
8. If a black-and-white hen (lay) eggs, some of her chicks (be) black, some white and some black-and-white.

66. Conditions that existed in the past (2.3.6)

Five years ago, the government of the People's Republic of Gloom made a Five Year Plan which has now failed – nothing happened as the government wanted it to!

Below are some of the points in the plan. How might the government talk about their failures now?

1. find oil in the Brown Sea – we can raise the standard of living
   (= If we had found oil in the Brown Sea, we could have raised the standard of living.)
2. start a thousand new factories – everybody will have a job
3. build 50,000 new houses – everybody will have a home
4. persuade farmers to grow more corn – nobody will be short of food
5. cut taxes – people will have more money to spend
6. train more doctors – we can improve the nation's health
7. throw away our nuclear arms – we will show that we want peace
8. carry out our Five Year Plan – we will make history!

67. Real conditions (2.3.6)

Below you can see the draw for a tennis championship. A commentator is talking about what various players have to do or can do.

Choose a clause from **B** to match each of the five clauses in **A**. Put the verbs in brackets into the correct form.

Example:

1. If Doreen and Angela Cross each win one more match, two sisters will play each other in the final.

Round 1	Semi-finals	Final
Angela Cross v. Janina Spassky	Angela Cross 6–0, 6–0	
Wendy King v. Maria Gonzales (the present champion)		
Eva di Stefano v. Ingrid Bernstein		
Helen Solkova v. Doreen Cross	Doreen Cross 6–4, 7–5	

A	B
1. If Doreen and Angela Cross each (win) one more match,	she (meet) Angela Cross in the semi-finals.
2. If Eva di Stefano (beat) Ingrid Bernstein and Doreen Cross,	she (become) champion without losing a single game.
3. If Wendy King (defeat) Maria Gonzales,	she (reach) the final.
4. If Maria Gonzales (succeed) in winning the final,	two sisters (play) each other in the final.
5. If Angela Cross (win) her next match 6–0, 6–0,	she (remain) champion for another year.

68. Mixed conditionals (2.3.6)

Gloria Wells likes Alan Speedy and feels sure he is soon going to invite her to go out with him.

Complete her thoughts by making correct forms of the verbs in brackets.

1. If he (come) into the canteen at lunchtime today, I hope he (sit) down at my table.
   (= If he comes into the canteen at lunchtime today, I hope he'll sit down at my table.)
2. If he (not be) so shy, he (ask me out) long ago.
3. If he (see) me coming out of work last Friday, he (probably speak) to me then.
4. If I (not go) home by bus tonight, there (be) more chance of our meeting.
5. If he (invite) me to go to the cinema with him tonight, I (may say) no.
6. And if he (want) to go to a pub, I (probably make) an excuse for not going, too.
7. But I (accept) if he (ask) me to go dancing.
8. If he (pay) for everything on our first date, it (be) my turn to pay the second time.
9. If he (take me out) three or four times, I (ask) him home to meet Mother.
10. If Mother (like) him, he (be able to come) and visit me any time.
11. Even if Mother (not like) him, I (not stop) seeing him.
12. If only he (comb) his hair more often, he (look) really smart.
13. His fingers (not be) so brown and ugly, either, if he (not smoke).
14. I wonder how old he is. If he (be) in Julia's class at school in 1983, he (must be) at least twenty now.

69. Direct and indirect speech (2.3.7 to 2.3.10)

Using the direct speech in the pictures as a guide, complete the indirect speech.

Direct speech   Indirect speech

1. As Tom went out, Mary asked him ____.

2. Tom told her that ____.

3. While Tom was out, the woman next door asked Mary ____.

4. Mary explained that ____.

5. When Tom came home, the man next door asked him ____.

6. Tom replied that ____.

70. Direct and indirect speech (2.3.7 to 2.3.10)

Liz Grey has told her father she wants to marry Ron, whom he does not know very well. As Mr Grey questions his daughter, Mrs Grey listens in the next room and tells Ron what she hears.

Write down what Mrs Grey says to Ron.

1. Are you thinking of marrying him very soon?
No.
What was that?
He asked Liz whether she was thinking of marrying you very soon, and she said she wasn't.

2. Does he really love you?
Yes.

3. Can you always trust him?
Yes.

4. Is he a kind man?
Yes.

5. Are you sure he earns enough money?
No.

6. Will you carry on working?
Yes.

7. Do his parents know he wants to marry you?
I don't know.

8. Have you found somewhere to live?
No.

9. Does he have many friends?
Yes.

10. Do you both love children?
I do, but Ron doesn't.

71. Indirect imperatives (2.3.11)

Mr Terry is complaining about things his children have done.
   Write what he said in reply to the following.

1. Tommy: Dad, I've knocked some paint off the
            car. I was riding my bike near it.
            **(= Mr Terry: I told you not to ride
            your bike near the car, Tommy!)**
2. Mary: Dad, the washing line's come down. I
            was pulling it.
3. Lenny: Dad, I've broken the kitchen window. I
            was playing football under it.
4. Tracy: Dad, Michael's walked on your garden.
            He was chasing the dog round it.
5. Tommy: Dad, I've cut my finger on your knife. I
            was cutting wood with it.
6. Lenny: Dad, the cat's drowning in the fish
            pond! We were teaching it to swim in it.
7. Mary: Dad, I've burnt my finger on the electric
            fire. I was making toast on it.
8. Tracy: Dad, Mary's torn her skirt on the tree.
            She was climbing up it.
9. Tommy: Dad, my watch has stopped. I was
            washing it.
10. Lenny: Dad, the front door won't open. I locked
            it with the garage key.

72. Indirect imperatives (2.3.11)

Jenny Gee is a gossip columnist. She gets her information from people she calls 'reliable sources'. Here is what one source told her. What do you think Jenny wrote? Continue from the example.

"Don't mention my name, darling, but I can tell you why June Wonda has stopped making her new film. I was listening to her doctor when he said, 'June, you must take a long break!' Then June went to the director of her film, Sam Hill, and said 'Sam, please let me have a rest.' His reply was short and sharp: 'Get back on the set!' and he added, 'Don't forget who's paying you to make the film!'
   June began to cry and her co-star Willy Sprout shouted at Hill, 'Don't come on so heavy, Sam! Let's all sleep on the problem before we decide anything.'
   But next morning Sam Hill hadn't changed his mind one bit. 'Take your holiday', he demanded. 'And my advice is, go as far away from me as you can get. Take Willy with you – and don't come back!' End of story, Jenny. Off they went!"

WHERE IS WONDA? by Jenny Gee
One of my reliable sources asked ¹___ (= **me not to mention**) her name, but said she could tell me why June Wonda had stopped making her new film. It seems her doctor had advised ²___. So June went to her director, Sam Hill, and asked ³___. Sam just ordered ⁴___ and told ⁵___. There and then June's co-star, Willy Sprout, told Hill ⁶___ and proposed ⁷___ before deciding anything. But next morning Hill demanded ⁸___, and advised ⁹___ as she could get. He also suggested ¹⁰___ and told ¹¹___!

---

73. Indirect speech (2.3.8 to 2.3.11)

After seeing some plays by Shakespeare, you decided to make notes of some of the important lines in your diary, but couldn't remember the exact words.

Below you can see the characters who spoke, and their words as you remembered them. In your diary you wrote them in indirect speech, like the example. Continue, using some or all of these words:

advise	ask	be afraid	beg	promise
say	swear	tell		warn	wonder

1. *Hamlet to himself:* Is it better for me to go on living or shall I end my life?

   (= Hamlet wondered whether it was better for him to go on living or whether he should end his life.)
2. *Witches to Macbeth:* Macbeth! You'll be king one day!
3. *Juliet to Romeo:* Romeo, Romeo, where are you?
4. *Polonius to his son:* Don't borrow money and don't lend it; because if you lend money, you'll lose it, and you'll lose your friend as well.
5. *Ghost to Hamlet:* Hamlet, I'm your father's ghost.
6. *Mark Antony to the crowd:* Everyone, listen to me – I've come to say a few words about Caesar, now that he's dead.
7. *Macbeth to himself:* Is it a knife I can see in front of me?
8. *Fortune-teller to Caesar:* Caesar! Be careful on the 15th March – someone's going to kill you!
9. *Hamlet to his father's ghost:* I'll kill the person who murdered you!
10. *Juliet to herself:* What's that light outside my window?

74. Clauses with infinitives and participles (2.3.12 to 2.3.13)

Mark and Sid, regional managers of Finelux Stores, are planning how to welcome Rita Hay, their Managing Director.

Make the correct infinitive or participle form from the words in brackets.

Mark: She's the most important person ever (^{1} visit) **(= to visit)** our region, Sid. So I want every branch (^{2} be) prepared. We must make her (^{3} feel) that we're doing a good job.

Sid: I agree. We don't want her to leave here (^{4} think) we're useless, do we? What time is she expected (^{5} arrive)?

Mark: I'm waiting for head office (^{6} tell) us. But she's likely (^{7} arrive) by air.

Sid: Whenever she comes, we'd better not keep her (^{8} wait). Anyway, why don't you let me (^{9} look after) the arrangements at the airport? It's no use (^{10} try) (^{11} do) everything yourself.

Mark: Thanks. You can help me (^{12} arrange) the reception at the airport. Do you think it would be worth (^{13} get) the managers from all our branches (^{14} line up) at the airport when she arrives?

Sid: No – I mean, can you imagine them all (^{15} stand) at the airport? If I were her, I'd prefer (^{16} find) the managers (^{17} wait) in their own branches, ready (^{18} show) me around. Though of course, she probably won't have enough time (^{19} visit) every branch.

Mark: Maybe not. But we'd better warn them all (^{20} be) ready, so that they know what (^{21} do) if she does come.

75. Infinitive clauses (2.3.12)

John Tremble wants a job, but he hasn't filled in his
application form very well. He has given the form to a
clerk who is complaining about all the missing
information and mistakes.

Application for employment

Name _John Tremble_

Address _____

Telephone number _____

Age _____

Number of children _____

References   1) _____

_____

2) _____

_____

Date _John Tremble_

Type of work wanted _____

Please tick factory you wish to work at

☐   ☐   ☐

Oxton   Barford   Selham

Last employer _____

_____

When can you start work? _____

General interests _____

_____

_____ (applicant's signature)

Complete John Tremble's answers to these complaints
which the clerk made. You have to choose one of the
words in brackets.

1. Clerk: You haven't put down the type of work
   you want.
   John: Sorry. I didn't know (what/who) ____.
   (= what to put down.)
2. Clerk: You've signed the form in the wrong
   place.
   John: Sorry. I didn't know (where/when) ____.
   (= where to sign it.)
3. Clerk: You haven't mentioned your last
   employer.
   John: Sorry. I didn't know (who/what) ____.
4. Clerk: You haven't dated your application.
   John: Sorry. I didn't know (when/where) ____.
5. Clerk: You haven't named anyone as a referee.
   John: Sorry. I didn't know (who/what) ____.

6. Clerk: You haven't suggested a date for starting
   work.
   John: Sorry. I didn't know (when/where) ____.
7. Clerk: You haven't ticked the factory you want to
   work at.
   John: Sorry. I couldn't decide (which/who) ____.
8. Clerk: You haven't given us a telephone
   number.
   John: Sorry. I didn't know (whose/whom) ____.
9. Clerk: You haven't filled in the 'general interests'
   part.
   John: Sorry. I didn't know (how/who) ____.
10. Clerk: You haven't said where you live.
    John: Sorry. I didn't know (where/when) ____.
11. Clerk: You haven't given us your age.
    John: Sorry. I couldn't remember (what age/
    what time) ____.
12. Clerk: You haven't written anything in the
    'number of children' space.
    John: Sorry. I wasn't sure (how many/how
    much) ____.

76. *For* + noun phrase + *to* + infinitive (2.3.12)

Someone in an advertising agency is writing an advertisement for holidays abroad. Complete it from these rough notes.

Examples:
Six different countries for you to holiday in!
No arrangements for you to make!

Holidaymakers can
– holiday in 6 different countries
– pick from 10 different fortnights
– travel on 3 different airlines
– choose from 12 outward and return flights
– stay at 24 different hotels
– see many fascinating national festivals
– take part in local music and dancing
– buy all sorts of gifts and bargains
– return home with lots of duty-free goods

and they don't have to
– make any arrangements
– fill in any complicated forms
– pay for any extra items

77. *Not* + Adj + *enough to* + infinitive; *not enough* + noun + *to* + infinitive (2.3.12)

Look at the pictures and make two sentences about each of them, using the table.

There is not enough		cotton
		snow
		string
		sun
		water
		wind
					to get a suntan.
					to sew the
					    button on with.
					to float the
					    canoe.

The	snow string sun water wind	is not	bright deep long strong	enough	to make a snowman. to fly the kite. to tie the parcel.

1.

2.

3.

4.

5.

6.

78. *Too* + Adj; *not* + Adj + *enough* (2.3.12)

First of all, fill in the squares according to the instructions. The first two instructions have been carried out for you.

	A	B	C	D	
1	–	–	·	–	= Q
2					
3					
4					
5					
6					
7					
8					

If an elephant is too big to pick up with one hand, put a dash (–) in 1A, 1B and 1D, and a dot (·) in 1C.
If a dog isn't fast enough to catch a rabbit, put a dash in 2C and a dot in 2D. (= *Do nothing – a dog is fast enough to catch a rabbit*)
If the sun is too hot to visit, put a dot in 2B and 2C, and a dash in 2D.
If the moon is too small to see, put a dash in 3B, and dots in 3C and 3D.
If eggs aren't strong enough to jump on, put a dot in 3D.
If wood is too hard to eat, put dots in 4B, 4C and 4D.
If the stars in the sky are too many to count, put a dash in 5D.
If your parents are too young to have any children, put a dash in 5C and a dot in 5D.
If the sea is warm enough for fish to live in, put dots in 6C and 6D.
If gold is cheap enough for people to make cooking pots with, put a dash in 6A and dots in 6B, 6C and 6D.
If the world is too big to walk round in one day, put dashes in 7B, 7C and 7D.
If ice is too cold to sit on comfortably in a swimming suit, put a dash in 8C and a dot in 8D.
If birds are usually too small to sit in trees, put a dot in 8B and 8C, and a dash in 8D.

Now you have finished the puzzle you can find the word which is hidden in it in Morse Code (see below). Each horizontal line in the puzzle represents a letter. So line 1 represents the letter Q.
   If you read the letters vertically you will find the hidden word.

The Morse Code

A	· –	N	– ·
B	– · · ·	O	– – –
C	– · – ·	P	· – – ·
D	– · ·	Q	– – · –
E	·	R	· – ·
F	· · – ·	S	· · ·
G	– – ·	T	–
H	· · · ·	U	· · –
I	· ·	V	· · · –
J	· – – –	W	· – –
K	– · –	X	– · · –
L	· – · ·	Y	– · – –
M	– –	Z	– – · ·

79. Adverbial clauses of time shortened by use of participles (2.3.13)

Below are some instructions for planting a rose bush.
   Rewrite each instruction, using the words in brackets.

5. Fill in the hole. Tread the soil down well. (after)

6. Put in a stick to support the rose. Water it well. (after)

1. Cut any dead branches off the rose. Then take it out of the plastic bag. (before)
(= Cut any dead branches off the rose before taking it out of the plastic bag.)

2. Dig a hole. Then put some fertilizer in the bottom. (after)
(= After digging a hole, put some fertilizer in the bottom.)

7. Check roses for damage by greenfly. Then choose the best ones for display. (before)

8. Cut roses. Then remove any thorns still on the stems. (after)

3. Take the bush out of the plastic bag. Then plant it in the hole. (before)

4. Test the height of the rose. Then fill the hole in. (before)

9. Take off any unwanted leaves. Arrange the flowers in a vase of water. (before).

---

80. Participial clauses (2.3.13)

Write each pair of sentences as one, by changing the verb in one of the sentences into its present or perfect participle form.

1a. Jack looked through the window. He saw a crocodile on the bed.
   (= Looking through the window, Jack saw a crocodile on the bed.)
1b. He cleaned the window. He climbed down the ladder again.
   (= Having cleaned the window, he climbed down the ladder again.)
1c. He wondered if the crocodile had escaped. He phoned the zoo.
2a. Mary and Dave were walking in the fields. They saw lots of sheep with their lambs.
2b. They went several miles. They sat down for a rest.
3a. Gill lost her key. She couldn't get into her flat.
3b. She sat on the doorstep. She felt cold and unhappy.
3c. She spent an hour sitting on the doorstep. She decided to ask the police for help.
4a. Andy returned to the office late one evening. He surprised a burglar.
4b. The burglar had cut himself breaking a window. He was trying to tie up his bleeding hand with a piece of curtain.
4c. Andy thought the burglar was going to attack him. He threw a telephone at his head.
5a. The mad king felt he was in danger. He had everyone in his family put to death.
5b. He killed all his relatives. He took his own life.

81. Adverbial clauses of time and reason (2.3.3)

Rewrite each of your answers from Exercise 80, so that it begins with *When, While, After* or *Because*.

1a. Looking through the window, Jack saw a crocodile on the bed.
   (= When he looked/While he was looking through the window, Jack saw a crocodile on the bed.)
1b. Having cleaned the window, he climbed down the ladder again.
   (= After he had cleaned the window, he climbed down the ladder again.)
1c. Wondering if the crocodile had escaped, he phoned the zoo.
   (= Because he wondered if the crocodile had escaped, he phoned the zoo.)

82. Participial clauses after verbs like *see, hear* (2.3.13)

A newspaper gave this information about entertainments on a certain day. Five visitors to London that day each did something different, and then wrote a postcard home to tell someone about it.

One postcard is given to you as an example. Write the other four.

1. Vicki did something at 1530 and 1930 and then wrote to her mother.
2. Silvia did something at 1230 and 1945 and then wrote to her mother.
3. Masako did something at 0930 and 2030 and then wrote to her sister Tachako.
4. Lars did something at 1600 and 2130 and then wrote to his father.
5. Ibrahim did something at 1430 and 1830 and then wrote to his brother Ali.

WHAT'S ON IN AND AROUND TOWN TODAY . . .

Films and plays
1830 James Moon stars as the famous agent in '008's Revenge', at the Odeon.
1945 Terry Craven plays Romeo and Hilary Sellers plays Juliet in 'Romeo and Juliet', at the Old Vic.

Sport
1430 The famous horse 'Rainbow' runs in the George Cup, at Epsom.
2130 Buster Clodd fights Bruno Orsini for the World Light-weight Boxing title, at the Albert Hall.

Music
1230 The Band of the Irish Guards plays lunch-hour music, in Green Park.
1930 Axel Petersen conducts the London Symphony Orchestra in Beethoven's Fifth Symphony, at the Barbican.
2030 Maria Wolf sings Carmen, at Covent Garden.

Other events
0930 Bill Lightfinger copies a painting by Van Gogh, at the Tate Gallery.
1530 The Queen opens Parliament.
1600 Professor Crunch explains the use of computers in ship design, at the Science Museum.

London, Friday

Dear Mum,
Today I watched the Queen opening Parliament in the afternoon, and I heard Axel Petersen conducting the London Symphony Orchestra in Beethoven's Fifth Symphony at the Barbican in the evening.
Love, Vicki

83. *Have something done* (2.3.13)

Look at the pictures and complete the sentences.

1. The hairdresser is cutting the man's hair.
   The man . . .
   (= The man is having his hair cut.)

2. The nurse is taking the patient's temperature.
   The patient . . .

3. The doctor is testing the boy's eyes.
   The boy . . .

4. The mechanic is repairing the old lady's car.
   The old lady . . .

5. The dressmakers are altering the customers' dresses.
   The customers . . .

Section three:

The verb phrase

84. Present simple: positive statements (3.2.1)

Mrs Robinson is writing a letter to her grandson Tim, to thank him for a kitten he gave her. Write each verb with the correct present simple verb ending.

I want to thank you for the lovely kitten. I ([1] call) (= **call**) her Sheba and she ([2] have) (= **has**) some lovely ways.

She always ([3] come) when I ([4] call) her, and when I ([5] open) a tin of cat food she always ([6] hurry) to eat it. Then, when she has finished her milk, she ([7] jump) onto my lap.

If you ([8] hang) a piece of string in front of her she always ([9] try) to catch it. Sometimes she ([10] play) with a little rubber mouse if I ([11] throw) it in front of her. But she ([12] scratch) people who ([13] pull) her tail too hard! And when children ([14] come), she usually ([15] go) out of the room. I think she's afraid of them.

On warm days she ([16] lie) outside in the garden. Sometimes she ([17] watch) the birds for hours, but she never ([18] catch) any of them.

When Mrs Ross, the cleaner, is working here, Sheba often ([19] chase) the vacuum cleaner. But Mrs Ross says she's the best cat in the world, and all of us here ([20] agree) with her.

85. Present simple: questions (3.2.1)

Rita, a reporter for Music News, is interviewing Lou Belize, who writes songs and sings for a successful pop group.

Fill in the blanks in the questions Rita asks.

Rita: Tell me, Lou, where [1]____ you ____ (= **do you write**) your songs?

Lou: Well, I write a lot of them in hotels and on buses. Anywhere, really.

Rita: [2]____ any other members of the group ____ songs?

Lou: Yes. Simon, the guitarist, writes some.

Rita: And how [3]____ you ____ if a song is good enough?

Lou: We decide together, after we've tried it out.

Rita: How long [4]____ it ____ you to write a song?

Lou: It varies. Sometimes it takes only minutes, but sometimes it takes days and days.

Rita: And where [5]____ the ideas for your songs ____ from?

Lou: Often they come from newspapers, things I've read about.

Rita: [6]____ the members of the group ____ a lot of time together, outside performances and the recording studios?

Lou: No, we don't really spend much time together. We like to be on our own when we can.

Rita: What [7]____ your mother ____ of your success?

Lou: Oh, she thinks it's wonderful.

Rita: [8]____ she ____ your songs?

Lou: Not really. She likes other kinds of music.

86. Present simple: negative statements (3.2.1)

Lucy and Cindy share a flat with some other girls. But they live different kinds of lives, and think differently about everything.

First, read what Lucy thinks.

1. I like it here.
2. The girls in the flat help each other.
3. We get on very well with each other.
4. I stay here at weekends.
5. My friends often come to visit me here.
6. My boyfriend lives in this part of town.
7. The things I see from my window interest me.
8. I have interesting conversations with the other girls.
9. They cook for me when I'm busy.
10. The local shops sell all the things I need.

Now find out what Cindy thinks, by changing all the sentences into their negative form.

87. Present simple: questions; positive and negative statements (3.2.1)

As part of a survey you have been collecting information about people's eating habits. You can see one of the filled-in questionnaires below.

What questions did you ask? What answers did you receive?

Example:
1. **You: How many meals do you have each day?**
   Interviewee: I usually have three.

---

1. Number of meals? *usually 3*
2. Biggest meal? *in the evening*
3. Meals in restaurants? *only if invited*
4. Who with?
   4a. Breakfast *alone*
   4b. Lunch *usually with friends from office*
   4c. Evening meal *family*
5. Kind of drink?
   5a. with breakfast *coffee*
   5b. with lunch *soft drinks*
   5c. with evening meal *water, sometimes wine*
6. Meat? *never*
7. Potatoes or rice? *rice*
8. Bread with every meal? *yes*

---

88. Present simple: negative questions (3.2.1)

Doris, who always complains a lot, is talking to her friend Alison. Each time Doris mentions a problem, Alison thinks what Doris should do (*She should . . .*) and then expresses it as a suggestion (*Why don't you . . . ?)* Write what Alison says.

1. 'I feel so tired all the time.'

> She should see a doctor.

'Why don't you see (= a doctor?')

2. 'I haven't had any breakfast.'

> We should go and have a cup of coffee.

3. 'I don't earn enough.'

> She should change her job.

4. 'My husband can't find a comfortable pair of shoes.'

> He should try Dixon's.

5. 'My son has had a quarrel with his girlfriend.'

> He should phone her and put things right.

6. 'I hate waiting for buses.'

> She should buy a small car.

7. 'I'll be all alone in the house tonight.'

> She should come and watch television with me.

8. 'My sons get so bored in the holidays.'

> They should join a youth club.

89. Present progressive with present reference: statements and questions (3.2.2)

Les has just met another student, Adrian, outside the student club.

Complete their conversation, using a present progressive form of the verb given in each sentence.

Les: Hello, Adrian. (^{1} you wait) **(= Are you waiting)** for someone?
Adrian: Yes. (^{2} Carol attend) a meeting in the club.
Les: I didn't know she was keen on sport.
Adrian: Oh, but she is. (^{3} she plan) to run in a marathon in August.
Les: (^{4} she train) very hard for it?
Adrian: I'll say! In fact, (^{5} she hope) to run twenty miles this evening, after the meeting.
Les: Good for her! But why don't you take more exercise yourself? (^{6} you put on) weight, you know!
Adrian: (^{7} I try) to lose weight by playing snooker.
Les: Snooker? That's not real exercise. I play squash.
Adrian: But squash is a killing game. (^{8} you look for) an early death?
Les: Don't be silly! (^{9} we not try) to be champions or anything like that. (^{10} we just keep) fit, that's all.
Adrian: What (^{11} you do) this morning?
Les: (^{12} I wait) for Jenny. (^{13} she write) some letters for the club. (the club organize) a big end-of-term dinner, you know.
Adrian: Careful, Les. You'll put on weight, too!

90. Present progressive: positive and negative statements (3.2.2)

The pictures below show what certain people usually do during their working hours, and what they are doing at this moment.
    Complete each sentence with the verbs given.

Usually   *At this moment*

type   drink

1. Sheila is a typist. But she ____ (= **isn't typing**) letters at the moment. She ____ (= **'s drinking**) coffee.

Usually   *At this moment*

perform   dig

2. Jane and Sue are actresses. However, this evening they ____ the garden. They ____ at the theatre.

Usually   *At this moment*

walk   play

3. Larry and I are policemen. But this afternoon we ____ up and down the streets. We ____ football for the police team.

Usually   *At this moment*

fly   decorate

4. Angela is a pilot. She ____ today, though. She ____ her flat.

Usually   *At this moment*

paint   check

5. Mark is a painter. But at the moment he ____ his bank statement. He ____ pictures.

91. Present progressive: negative statements and questions (3.2.2)

A group of apprentices are on a training course. It is a very hard course, and some of them are starting to feel tired.

Make present progressive negative statements and questions from the words given below.

Lewis, (¹ you not do) **(= you aren't doing)** your work! Why (² you not tighten) those screws?

(⁵ I not get) anywhere with this course. Why (⁶ I not lie) on the beach? Or playing football?

Why (⁷ that apprentice not repair) the machine? (⁸ He not do) what I told him to do.

(³ we not have) a break today, Mr. Grimes?

No. (⁴ we not have) a break till everyone has done today's project.

Why (⁹ you not work) with the others, Charlie? Why (¹⁰ Alan and Jill not help) you?

(¹¹ they not do) the same project, Mr Grimes.

92. Present progressive and present simple (3.2.3 to 3.2.5)

The staff at Finefashions Ltd are all doing different things during the holidays.

Choose the verb which has the right meaning in each blank, and write its correct form. The verbs in brackets are sometimes in the right order, and sometimes not.

1. Jeff ____ (= **likes**) sailing, so he ____ (= **is taking out**) a boat with some friends. (take out/like)
2. Maria ____ a week in Italy because she ____ Italian relatives. (have/spend)
3. Barry and Kate ____ cold, wet weather. Because of this they ____ to Spain, where it's sure to be warm. (fly/hate)
4. I ____ some friends in the north of Scotland, because I hardly ever ____ the chance to see them. (get/visit)
5. Phil ____ chess whenever he can, so he ____ a chess competition. (play/take part in)
6. Jenny ____ to Greece by train because she ____ about flying on planes. (worry/travel)
7. John, the manager, ____ a lot of heavy business lunches. So he ____ at a health farm, to lose weight. (eat/spend some time)
8. June ____ to a choir, and during her holiday she ____ with them in a music festival in Germany. (sing/belong)
9. Lawrence ____ poems in his spare time. He ____ to organize a series of poetry readings. (help/write)
10. Tessa ____ a party of climbers up Snowdon because she ____ extra money. (need/guide)

93. Present progressive; present simple; *can* + *see/hear* (3.2.3 to 3.2.5)

Alan is writing to Dave, an old friend from his student days.

Make a suitable verb form from the words in brackets, choosing between present simple, present progressive, and *can* + *see/hear*.

Forth House,
Pentland.

Dear Dave,

I (¹ write) because as you (² see) we now (³ have) a new address. We moved here, near Edinburgh, about two months ago. Perhaps you (⁴ remember) that I used to work in Newcastle. Anyway, I wasn't very happy there, so now I (⁵ work) for a small electronics firm in this area.

Why (⁶ you not come) and spend a holiday with us here this summer? Our house (⁷ stand) on the edge of the hills, and on a clear day you (⁸ see) the mountains 80 miles away. We (⁹ not have) any of the city dirt and smells up here, and usually all you (¹⁰ hear) are the sounds of birds and sheep. We (¹¹ spend) a lot of time gardening. This year we (¹² grow) potatoes.

And what (¹³ you do) these days? (¹⁴ you still work) for the same firm? It's sad that we (¹⁵ not seem) to keep in touch the way we used to, but if you (¹⁶ come) and (¹⁷ see) us in the summer we (¹⁸ hear) all each other's news.

Yours ever,

Alan

94. Past simple: positive statements (3.3.1)

A video shop puts up descriptions (in the present tense) to help its customers choose which videos to borrow.

Imagine that you have seen the four videos below. Tell the stories to a friend, this time using the past tense.

The soldiers swear to rescue their comrades. They ride across deserts, cut their way through jungles and swim across flooded rivers. At last they come to the enemy fort. They creep past the sentries, burst into the enemy headquarters and blow up the prison!

Frank thinks that Emma no longer loves him. He decides to forget her. But then someone tells him that Emma is a prisoner in her uncle's house. The messenger brings a letter in which Emma begs Frank to help her. Frank drives to the village and makes enquiries. He hears that the house is well guarded.

A spacecraft from Earth lands on a distant planet and a gang of robots meet it. The robots know that there are men and women in the spacecraft. They seek to enter it by any means. The whole spacecraft shakes as the robots strike it with rocks and beat on it with their metal claws. Then they begin to cut open the door with an electric torch, and the door gives way.

A wizard teaches magic to his apprentice, Hobo, for many years. But Hobo is secretly jealous of his master's powers. The wizard keeps a book of magic spells in his cupboard. One day Hobo steals the book while his master is asleep. The wizard wakes up and flies after Hobo on his magic carpet. Hobo is so frightened that he loses the book while crossing a river.

95. Past simple: questions answered by positive and negative statements (3.3.1)

Before his wife Mary went away on business for a week, Basil wrote a list of jobs he intended to do while she was away. Here is the list:

feed the cat	take Mary's books back to the library
clean the windows	
paint the fence	put up the bookshelves in Sandra's room
water the plants	dig the garden

When Mary came back, she asked Basil if he had done everything. Complete the conversation.

Mary: ¹___ (= **Did you feed)** the cat?
Basil: Yes, ²___ (= **I fed)** it every day.
Mary: Well done! ³___ the plants?
Basil: Well, no. At least, ⁴___ them every day.
Mary: ⁵___ the windows?
Basil: Yes, ⁶___ them on Tuesday.
Mary: Good. ⁷___ the fence?
Basil: No, ⁸___ it. It was raining all the time.
Mary: ⁹___ the bookshelves in Sandra's room?
Basil: Yes, ¹⁰___ them up yesterday. But they fell down again this morning.
Mary: ¹¹___ my books back to the library?
Basil: Sorry. ¹²___ them back because I couldn't find them.
Mary: Bother! Now I'll have to pay a fine. I suppose you didn't have time to dig the garden?
Basil: Yes, I did. In fact, ¹³___ it the day you left.

96. Past simple: positive and negative statements and questions (3.3.1)

There has been a crime and Paul Adams saw the man who did it. Inspector Moss finds his story hard to believe.

Change the verb phrases *in italics* to the correct form, but if they are already correct, like the first one, leave them unchanged. Add negatives where necessary.

Moss: Now, Mr Adams, let's go over your story again. ¹ *You stayed* at home all Monday night. Is that right?
Adams: That's right.
Moss: And at seven o'clock ² *you noticed* a man coming out of the building opposite.
Adams: Yes.
Moss: How ³ *the man came out* of the building?
Adams: ⁴ *He climbed out* of a downstairs window.
Moss: What ⁵ *he looked* like?
Adams: I can't really describe him.
Moss: Why not? ⁶ *You saw* his face?
Adams: No. It was hidden by the collar of his coat.
Moss: I see. Where ⁷ *he went* then?
Adams: I don't know. ⁸ *I paid* any attention.
Moss: Really? ⁹ *You thought* it strange when a man climbed out of a window like that?
Adams: But how ¹⁰ *I knew* he had committed a crime?
Moss: Surely ¹¹ *you suspected* something? That brings me to the question: why ¹² *you telephoned* the police when you saw him?
Adams: Well ¹³ *it seemed* to be any of my business.
Moss: Mm. I find your story rather strange. Are you sure ¹⁴ *you recognized* the man?

97. Past progressive and past simple (3.3.1 to 3.3.2)

Lisa and Bob have been married for ten years. This evening they are looking at some of their old photographs and talking about them.

   Join the notes together to find out what they say about each picture. Decide whether to use *when* or *while* and whether the word you choose should come at the beginning or in the middle of the sentence. Usually, more than one sentence is possible.

1. I (push) the pram –
   a bee (sting) me
   (**= While I was
   pushing the
   pram a bee
   stung me.**)

2. You (look after) the
   children – I (study)
   hard for my exams
   (**= While you were
   looking after the
   children, I was
   studying hard for
   my exams.**)

3. the Clarks (visit) us –
   a driver (crash) his
   car into our house

4. I (have) Meg – you
   (work) on an oil rig
   in the North Sea

5. Meg (learn) how to
   swim – you (teach)
   Billy to ride a bike

6. we (have) a meal
   outside – you (nearly
   swallow) a fishbone

7. you (drop) the
   paintpot on Billy –
   you (paint) the
   bedroom window

8. Meg (catch) a bad
   cold – she and I
   (stay) with Aunt Lucy

98. Present perfect: questions; positive and negative statements (3.4.1 to 3.4.2.1)

Jane Lyle of Penman Publishers is checking some matters with her secretary, Rose Fox.

Using the words in brackets, make present perfect verb forms.

Jane: Rose, (¹ you write) **(= have you written)** to Bold Books yet?

Rose: Yes, (² I send) them a letter, but (³ they not reply) so far.

Jane: Well, that's OK. Now, about the meeting tomorrow. (⁴ I telephone) Bradley, but (⁵ I not be able) to contact Earnshaw.

Rose: Don't worry, I'll phone him. By the way, (⁶ you book) the visitors' dining room for lunch today?

Jane: No, (⁷ I not make) any arrangements at all. People say the food at Jack's Inn is good.

Rose: Yes, (⁸ it always be) good when (⁹ I be) there. Jane, something's worrying me. (¹⁰ nobody tell) me when the sales conference is being held. (¹¹ anybody say) anything to you?

Jane: Oh, don't worry about that. Apparently (¹² Eileen not decide) yet about the exact dates. There's a problem about holidays.

Rose: I see. Just one more thing. (¹³ Reg Slim's wife phone) to say he won't be in today. She says (¹⁴ he not be) well for a day or two.

Jane: I'm sorry to hear that. It must be flu. (¹⁵ several people be) off work with it recently.

Rose: Yes, well, (¹⁶ I have) flu once already this year. I don't want it again!

99. Present perfect with the adverbs *already, yet, just, ever, never* (3.4.2.1 and 3.4.2.2) még – már

Ivor and Sarah are discussing travel plans.

Complete their conversation by using the correct forms of the verbs in brackets, and putting the adverbs in their correct places. Sometimes more than one answer is possible.

Ivor: Sarah, (¹ you think yet) about our next trip? **(= Sarah, have you thought about our next trip?)**

Sarah: I'd like to go to Brazil. (² you be ever) there?

Ivor: Yes, (³ I be already) there once. I visited Rio in 1981.

Sarah: But (⁴ you sail never) up the Amazon?

Ivor: No, but I don't much like holidays on boats. I'd prefer to go east. (⁵ you visit ever) Burma?

Sarah: No. (⁶ I fly) over it once or twice. But (⁷ I land never) there.

Ivor: As a matter of fact, (⁸ my cousin Albert come back just) from Burma. We could ask him about it.

Sarah: Mm, Burma would be lovely. But (⁹ we spend just) so much on the house. I wonder if we can really afford it.

Ivor: Perhaps you're right. Oh dear, there are so many countries (¹⁰ we not see yet).

Sarah: Yes. (¹¹ I finish just) a book about New Guinea. There are wonderful forests and mountains there and (¹² nobody explore yet) them properly. (¹³ I start already) to plan the journey in my mind!

100. Present perfect with *for* and *since* (3.4.2.3)

It is 1987 and Mr Leigh has found some of his old diaries and is telling a friend some things he and his relatives have or haven't done for some time.

Make two sentences from each of the sentences given, using *for* and *since*. Further notes are given to help you.

1. I moved to Horton in 1965 when I got married.
   (Use the verb live*)*
   (= a. I've lived in Horton for twenty-two years.
   b. I've lived in Horton since 1965.
      or: I've lived in Horton since I got married.)
2. My wife last saw her sister in 1970, when she went to live in Australia. (*Use a negative form*)
3. My father started collecting old coins in 1977, when he retired.
4. Jan, my daughter, met her boyfriend three years ago, when she began her studies at university. (*Use the verb* know)
5. I bought my present car in 1965, when I moved to Horton. (*Use the verb* own)
6. Aunt Lily stopped eating meat in 1967, when a doctor told her it was bad for her. (*Use a negative form*)
7. My mother gave up driving six years ago, when her eyesight failed. (*Use a negative form*)
8. I began to wear glasses eight years ago, when I started getting headaches at work.

101. Past simple and present perfect (3.3.1 and 3.4.2)

Wat Piston is an inventor. Read this article about one of his inventions. Make the correct form of the verb (past simple or present perfect) from the words in brackets.

Wat Piston, who last year ([1] receive) a prize for his invention of the Piston Gas Fire, ([2] now invent) a new type of steam engine. When I ([3] interview) him recently at his home in York he ([4] tell) me about it. 'I ([5] get) the idea from some work I ([6] do) many years ago for the Steam Preservation Society', he ([7] say). 'For years now, people ([8] think) that there is no future for steam as an everyday source of power. Indeed, after the railways ([9] stop) using steam engines people ([10] almost forget) about it. Yet steam ([11] be) the main source of power in this country for over 150 years, until World War Two. I ([12] always believe) that steam has a future as well as a past.'

Piston is a remarkable man who ([13] have) an unusual career. He ([14] leave) school when he was 15, and ([15] not have) any training as an engineer until he was 35. Yet now he ([16] design) a steam engine more efficient than any of the engines that ([17] be built) during the great age of steam. 'The engineers of the past ([18] be) great men', he says. 'But they ([19] not develop) the best possible steam engine. The techniques I ([20] invent) will change that.'

102. Present perfect progressive (3.4.3)

Lynn is talking to her son Thomas.
   Make correct verb forms in the present progressive, using the words in brackets.

Lynn: What ([1] you do) (= **have you been doing**), Thomas?
Thomas: ([2] I play) with Brian.
Lynn: Brian? Is that the boy ([3] who ring) our door-bell every day for the past week?
Thomas: Yes, Mum. ([4] we have) a great time.
Lynn: You don't look very clean. ([5] you play) in the scrapyard with those old cars again?
Thomas: Yes. ([6] we pretend) we're inventors.
Lynn: That's all very well. But ([7] I wash) clothes all morning. And now I'll have to start all over again. What's more, ([8] some of the neighbours complain) about the noise you make in the scrapyard.
Thomas: Well, ([9] Brian and I not do) anything noisy this morning.
Lynn: That's good. But you'd better not play there any more.
Thomas: OK, Mum. Can I bring Brian in now for something to eat?
Lynn: Do you mean ([10] he stand) outside the door all this time? All right. Bring him in.
Thomas: And can we go and play in the scrapyard this afternoon?
Lynn: ([11] you not listen) to anything ([12] I say)? No, you can't go there. And if I find ([13] you go) there, I'll tell your father, and we'll see what he has to say.

103. Mixed past and present perfect forms (3.3.1 to 3.4.3)

John is writing a love letter to Carla. You can read it below.
   Change the words in brackets into past or present perfect forms. Sometimes there is more than one possibility.

My darling Carla,

It ([1] be) so long since you ([2] go) away. I ([3] mark off) each day on the calendar, and it's already sixty-three!
   Last night I ([4] look) at the moon, and ([5] wonder) if you ([6] look) at it, too.
   All our friends ([7] ask) me when you will be back. They ([8] try) to cheer me up because they say I always look so sad! This morning, while I ([9] shave), the postman ([10] ring) the doorbell, and I immediately ([11] run) downstairs, because I ([12] hope) there would be a letter from you. But once again there ([13] be) nothing!
   Since you ([14] leave) there ([15] not be) a single day when I ([16] not think) of you. One or two other girls ([17] ask) me to take them out, but I ([18] always refuse). I ([19] tell) them I ([20] promise) you that I wouldn't ever go out with anyone else. Yesterday I ([21] listen) to the radio and I ([22] hear) 'Sweet emotion' – *our* song! I ([23] feel) like crying! We ([24] listen) to it the first time at Elbow's Disco, but I ([25] give) my heart to you long before that.
   With unending love, darling,
      Your John.

104. Past perfect and past perfect progressive (3.5.1 and 3.5.2)

Joe Morran was one of the few survivors when the S.S. Gigantic sank on its first voyage across the Atlantic.

Complete his story by putting the words in brackets into past perfect or past progressive forms.

It all seems like yesterday. Did you know that the newspapers (¹say) the Gigantic was unsinkable? The King himself (²launch) the ship, and we were all so proud of her. Everyone said she was the greatest ship that people (³ever build), anywhere or anytime.

And then I remember the voyage itself, and that terrible night. All evening the passengers (⁴enjoy) themselves. Some of them (⁵drink) champagne and others (⁶dance). And then came the horrifying crash.

Actually, it was just bad luck that we hit the iceberg. Another ship, the Luxor, (⁷pass) us only two hours earlier. Later I heard that it (⁸try) to warn us of the danger ahead, but its radio (⁹break down).

In fact, when we struck the iceberg we (¹⁰already sail) among small icebergs for half an hour and we (¹¹already reduce) speed. All the same, it seemed to rush at us out of the darkness. The look-out, who (¹²see) it first, tried to warn the captain, but by then it was too late.

105. Mixed past and perfect forms (3.3.1 to 3.5.2)

Complete this newspaper report by making correct verb forms from the words in brackets. Sometimes there is more than one possibility.

LOCAL COUPLE WIN LOTTERY PRIZE

Ron and Emma Wilson of Paisley (¹ have) a wonderful surprise last week. They (² discover) they (³ win) £200,000 in the Scottish National Lottery.

Emma (⁴ buy) tickets for the lottery for years, but until last week she (⁵ never win) anything.

She told our reporter: 'I (⁶ just talk) to Ron about our money problems when the postman (⁷ bring) the letter that (⁸ tell) us about our win. Of course, we're very happy!'

Until recently, Ron (⁹ work) at Oldfield Steelworks. But then an injury at work (¹⁰ force) him to retire. Indeed, the Wilsons (¹¹ think) of moving to a smaller house because their present house (¹² become) too expensive for them.

Emma said, 'All my life I (¹³ wonder) what it would be like to have enough money, and not have to count every penny. Now that this money (¹⁴ come along), it's like a miracle!'

The Wilsons (¹⁵ already decide) on some of the things they want to do with their prize. In fact, last week they (¹⁶ try) to buy a big new house, but the owner (¹⁷ already sell) it. 'Now we (¹⁸ start) to look for another one, somewhere near the place we love best, the Scottish Highlands.'

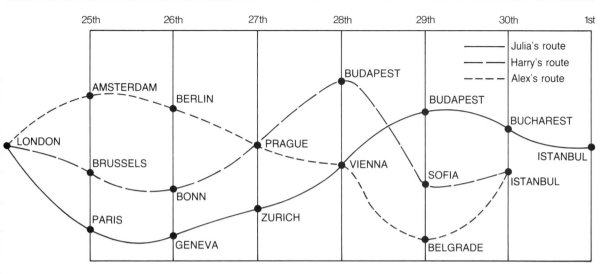

106. *Will*-future (3.6.1)

Three managers, Julia, Harry and Alex, have all planned trips from London to Istanbul, but by different routes. All three will start out on the same day, 24th June.

Make *Wh*-questions from the words given and then, after studying the routes, answer your own questions.

1. Julia/stay on 28th June
   **(= Where will Julia stay on 28th June?
   She'll stay in Vienna.)**
2. Alex/reach Berlin
   **(= When will Alex reach Berlin?
   He'll reach there on 26th June.)**
3. Julia/arrive in Istanbul
4. Alex/spend the night of 29th June
5. Harry and Alex/meet on the way to Istanbul
6. two routes/cross on 28th June
7. Julia/land in Budapest
8. Harry/wake up on 1st July
9. Alex/fly on from Berlin
10. Julia/join Harry and Alex in Istanbul

107. *Will*-future (3.6.1)

Nola is worried and Peter wants to cheer her up.

Complete Peter's part of the conversation, using the words given in brackets and either *'ll* or *won't* to complete the verb form.

Nola: I'm worried about my exams next week.
Peter: Don't worry, You (¹ fail). I'm sure you (² do) well.
Nola: Anyway, even if I pass them, my life (³ change). I'll still go on working in the same old job for the same old boss.
Peter: I know you don't like him, but don't worry. He probably (⁴ stay) much longer. He's not happy here. I expect he (⁵ leave) soon.
Nola: Well, let's think about something more pleasant. Shall we go away after the exam?
Peter: I (⁶ tell) you a good idea. We (⁷ spend) a few days at my aunt's cottage in Essex, where we went last summer. Remember?
Nola: I remember the accident you had on the way.
Peter: Oh, don't worry. I (⁸ have) an accident this time. And the car (⁹ break down), either. I've just had it serviced.
Nola: We (¹⁰ need) our sleeping bags. They're in the loft. I expect they're damp and dirty.
Peter: That's all right. I (¹¹ get them down) this evening, I (¹² wash) them in the morning, and then I (¹³ hang) them out in the garden to dry.

63

108. Future progressive with *will* (3.6.1)

Two elderly people, Harry and Barbara Duke, are home again after a long holiday in Australia. They will soon be back in the routines you see below.

1. Mondays: Harry sees his friends at the social club.

2. Tuesdays: Barbara helps at the Women's Institute.

3. Every morning: Barbara comes for coffee and a chat with her neighbour, Cathy.

4. Every evening: Harry takes the dog for a walk.

5. Fridays: both join their friends at the Crown for the weekly sing-song.

6. Thursdays: Barbara fetches her copy of Woman's World from the newspaper shop.

7. Saturdays: both watch their favourite TV programme, The Grunters.

8. Sundays: both attend morning service at St Mary's church.

What do Harry and Barbara say? What do their friends and neighbours say? Fill in the sentences below using future progressive forms.

1. Harry says, 'I ____' (= **I'll be seeing my friends at the social club again.)**
2. Harry says, 'Well, Barbara, you ____'
3. Cathy says, 'Barbara's back. She ____'
4. Barbara says, 'Harry, you ____'
5. Friends at the Crown say, 'Harry and Barb have come back. They ____'

6. The man in the newspaper shop says, 'I saw Mrs Duke today. She ____'
7. Harry and Barbara say, 'On Saturdays ____'
8. The vicar of St Mary's church met them in the street and said, 'Nice to see you again. You ____, won't you?'

109. *Will*-future and future progressive with *will* (3.6.1)

Ula and Pam are air hostesses. Ula has been chosen to fly on an interesting new route.

Change the words in brackets to the correct *will*-future or future progressive form. Sometimes both forms are possible.

Ula: Guess what, Pam! From next month (¹ I fly) (= **I'll be flying**) on the new London–Hong Kong route.

Pam: Well, that's exciting. (² you fly) via Dubai or via Bahrain?

Ula: Neither. (³ we stop) at Muscat, in Oman. (⁴ they probably ask) me to work on the first stage, London–Oman.

Pam: Do you know who (⁵ you fly) with?

Ula: I think (⁶ it be) Captain Bond. And if it is, I expect (⁷ he give) us a hard time.

Pam: Oh, he's OK. (⁸ you not have) any problems with him. But (⁹ you do) something for me?

Ula: What's that?

Pam: When you're in Oman, (¹⁰ you buy) some cloth for me? (¹¹ I pay) for it, of course.

Ula: OK. Of course, I don't know yet how long (¹² I stay) in Oman between flights. (¹³ I not be able) to go on any shopping trips immediately. But I'm sure (¹⁴ they give) us time for sightseeing eventually. (¹⁵ I certainly buy) some for you, if you can wait a while.

110. *Going to*-future (3.6.2)

On New Year's Day the Johnsons have each made a New Year's resolution and put it on the kitchen noticeboard to remind themselves and to tell other members of the family.

Complete their resolutions
(a) as they would tell them to others,
(b) as others would read them.

Example:
1(a) I'm going to help mother more around the house.

(b) Ron is going to help his mother more around the house.

111. *Going to*-future for future consequences of present situations (3.6.2)

If you want to be a pilot you have to take a test of your judgement in different situations. The tester shows you photographs and asks you what is going to happen.

Make the tester's questions with the words given in brackets, and answer them.

1. Look at the rescuer and the man in the icy water. (reach)
(= Is the rescuer going to reach the man in the icy water?
No, he isn't going to reach him.
Or = Yes, he is going to reach him.)

2. Look at the motor cyclists and the river. (fall into)

3. Look at the mouse and the cat. (escape from)

4. Look at runner number 36 and the winning line. (win)

5. Look at the bricks. (fall down)

6. Look at us in the maze. (get out)

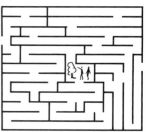

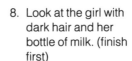

7. Look at the stone and the man underneath. (be killed)

8. Look at the girl with dark hair and her bottle of milk. (finish first)

112. *Will*-future; future progressive; *going to*-future (3.6.1 and 3.6.2)

Ted and Debby want to start a club for teenagers. They are talking about it with Leila, whose committee provides money for clubs.

Make *will*-future, future progressive or *going to* forms from the verbs in brackets. Sometimes more than one answer is possible.

Leila: So, Ted, Debby, I understand from your letter that you (¹ set up) a club.

Ted: Yes. We (² start) a club for teenagers in the community centre.

Leila: But isn't there a club in your area already?

Debby: Yes, but it (³ close down). The organizer is quite old, and he (⁴ retire) soon.

Leila: I see. But are you sure that you (⁵ get) permission to use the community centre?

Ted: Yes. We've been told that there (⁶ be) no problem.

Leila: OK. But if you go ahead with this plan, you (⁷ give) yourselves a lot of hard work. You realize that, don't you?

Debby: Oh yes. We know we (⁸ have to) spend a lot of time on it.

Leila: Right, then. I (⁹ not be able) to give you an answer for a few days. But later this week the members of my committee (¹⁰ have) their usual monthly meeting. I (¹¹ ask) them for some money to help you. If we give the money, we (¹² not interfere) with your running of the club. But we (¹³ expect) you to report to us regularly.

113. Future expressed through present progressive (3.6.4)

The Turners want to invite the Motsons (Tim, Brenda, Bob and Joyce) for dinner next week. But the Motsons have already made arrangements for almost every night of the week, as you can see from Tim Motson's diary.

Continue the phone conversation between John Turner and Tim Motson. Sunday is done for you.

Examples:

John: **I'd like to invite you all for dinner, Tim. Are you doing anything on Sunday evening?**

Tim: **I'm sorry. I'm taking part in a concert at the old people's home on Sunday evening.**

John: **What about Monday, then?**

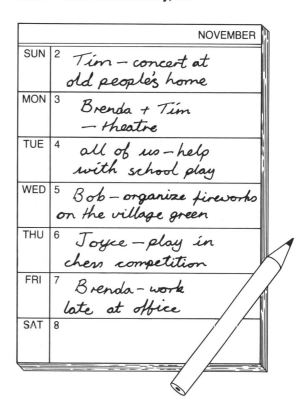

		NOVEMBER
SUN	2	Tim — concert at old people's home
MON	3	Brenda + Tim — theatre
TUE	4	all of us — help with school play
WED	5	Bob — organize fireworks on the village green
THU	6	Joyce — play in chess competition
FRI	7	Brenda — work late at office
SAT	8	

114. Future expressed through present simple (3.6.5)

Complete this advertisement for a sea cruise by using each of the verbs in the box once, in the correct form.

```
call   continue   depend   dress   get
give   go   last   meet   sail   see
spend   start   take   win
```

In the dark days of next winter – to be exact, on Friday 10th February – the party ¹___ at the Holton Hotel in West London, where it ²___ the first night. At dinner that evening everybody ³___ to know each other before our holiday ⁴___. Early next morning we ⁵___ the train to Tilbury where we ⁶___ on board our luxury liner, the S.S. 'Sardonic'. The liner ⁷___ at six o'clock that evening for the warm, tropical waters of the Caribbean. The voyage across the Atlantic ⁸___ six days, with fun all the way. For example, there is the fancy dress ball, when every passenger ⁹___ as a different historical character and everyone ¹⁰___ a prize! Then, our ship ¹¹___ first at Nassau in the Bahamas. The friendly faces there are world-famous; a welcoming party ¹²___ every lady enough flowers to fill her cabin! After two days the 'Sardonic' ¹³___ her voyage south to Kingston, Jamaica. Here we ¹⁴___ plantations of sugar, the crop on which the economy of this West Indian island ¹⁵___.

115. Future perfect (*will have done*) and future progressive (*will be doing*) (3.6.6 and 3.6.1)

Wendy is only 12, but already wants to become a famous writer. She spends hours dreaming about things she will be doing, or will have done, at various times in the future.

Complete the sentences below with the correct forms of the words in brackets.

1. By the end of this school year I (write) **(= 'll be writing)** really fast.
2. By the time I'm 13 I (finish) **(= 'll have finished)** the novel I'm going to start next week.
3. By the time I'm 14 I (sell) my first novel to a publisher.
4. By the time I'm 15 a television company (make) my first story into a film.
5. By the time I'm 20 I (appear) in my own show on television, and I (give) my opinion of other writers' work.
6. By the time I'm 25 I (produce) at least five best-sellers.
7. By the time I'm 30 I (not live) here in England.
8. By the time I'm 40, famous directors (film) most of my novels.
9. By the time I'm 50 people (call) me the Queen of the Novel.
10. By the time I'm 60 I (win) a lot of prizes for my novels.
11. By the time I die I (still not write) all the good stories in my head.

116. Using *is to/are to* to express future (3.6.6)

Expand the following newspaper headlines into full sentences. Remember to add articles as necessary.

1. BBC EXTENDING NINE O'CLOCK NEWS FROM JAN 1
   (= The BBC is to extend the nine o'clock news from 1st January.)
2. PRESIDENT NOT VISITING MOSCOW IN MAY
3. HOSPITALS NOT ALLOWING NURSES TO WEAR JEANS
4. PRICES GOING UP AGAIN NEXT YEAR
5. SECONDARY SCHOOLS INTRODUCING TEACHING OF CHINESE
6. PRINCESS SINGING IN POP CONCERT FOR FAMINE VICTIMS
7. LOBOWSKI NOT RECEIVING NOBEL PRIZE FOR PEACE
8. GOVERNMENT TAXING EARNINGS OF FOREIGN SPORTSMEN FROM DEC 31
9. AMERICAN AND RUSSIAN ASTRONAUTS LINKING UP IN SPACE ON FEB 3
10. EAST AND WEST SIGNING NUCLEAR TEST BAN ON TUESDAY

117. Mixed forms expressing the future (3.6.1 to 3.6.6)

In the two dialogues below, put the words in brackets into a future form. When more than one answer is possible, give one alternative answer, also.

(a) *Fay and Tom both work at a children's hospital.*

Tom: (¹ you go) **(= Are you going/Will you be going)** to the staff dance tomorrow night?
Fay: No. (² I take) some of the children to the seaside tomorrow, so (³ I not get back) in time. How about you? (⁴ you go)?
Tom: Oh yes. (⁵ I be) there.
Fay: And (⁶ you take) a partner?
Tom: No, I don't think (⁷ I ask) anyone to go with me.
Fay: Why not? Ask Jean. I'm sure (⁸ she not say no) if you ask her.

(b) *Lucy has passed an exam, but Joy has failed.*

Lucy: Bad luck, Joy. But never mind.
Joy: (⁹ it be) a busy summer for me now.
Lucy: The (¹⁰ next exam take place) in September. (¹¹ you try) again then?
Joy: Yes. (¹² I revise) something different each day of the holidays. You're lucky – (¹³ you lie) on the beach all the time!
Lucy: (¹⁴ you not take) any time off? Everybody needs a rest some time, you know.
Joy: I can't afford to. I expect (¹⁵ I study) for ever and (¹⁶ I still not pass) even in the year 2000!
Lucy: Don't be silly! I'm sure (¹⁷ you pass) in September.

118. *Be* as main verb; *there* + *be* (3.8.1 to 3.8.3)

Magicstore has been rebuilt and is going to reopen soon. Danny Lock, the manager, is talking to Sarah Bland, a reporter from the local radio station.

Make the correct form of *be* each time it occurs. When there is no subject, put in *there*.

Sarah: Well, this (¹ not be) **(= isn't)** Magicstore as I remember it. In fact, (² be) **(= there's)** a completely different feel about the place now. Tell me, Danny, (³ be) many changes to the building itself?

Danny: Yes, we've made a lot of changes. In fact, (⁴ be) a whole new wing which didn't exist before. It (⁵ be) our new 'Focus on Youth' department.

Sarah: And (⁶ be) any particular problems in all this reorganization?

Danny: Yes, (⁷ be) several difficulties, especially with the actual rebuilding, which is still going on. But we (⁸ be) sure that the store (⁹ be) ready to reopen in two weeks' time. (¹⁰ not be) any delays.

Sarah: Magicstore (¹¹ be) bigger in future. So (¹² be) more people on your staff?

Danny: Yes, indeed. (¹³ be) a lot of new faces in the store when we reopen.

Sarah: (¹⁴ be) time to see the new wing now? I'd like to take some photographs.

Danny: Oh, what a pity! It (¹⁵ be) open until five minutes ago, but the workmen have just gone home and locked it up. It (¹⁶ not be) open again now till tomorrow morning.

119. *Have* as main verb; *have* as action verb; *have got* (3.9.2 and 3.9.3)

Some of the staff of Supreme Sports Equipment are having a meal in a restaurant at the end of their Sales Conference.

Complete the dialogues. Make verb forms using the words in brackets together with a suitable form of *have* or *have got*. More than one answer may be possible.

(a) *Rose and Joe are looking at the menu*

Rose: Mm. (¹ They) **(= They have/They've got)** some pizzas with interesting names. 'Pizza Bella Palermo' – I think (² I) that. What (³ you), Joe?

Joe: (⁴ I) the fish. (⁵ I) a pizza here last week, and I didn't like it much.

(b) *Two sales directors, Helen and Alan, are talking*

Helen: (⁶ you) a look at Frank's report on his trip to Italy?

Alan: No, (⁷ I not) time to read it yet. In fact, (⁸ I not) a chance to read it until next week. (⁹ I) so much work at the moment with the Sales Conference, (¹⁰ I not) a moment for anything else.

(c) *Marie is talking to Dave about company gossip*

Marie: I hear Bill Clark has applied for a job with Merlin Sportswear. (¹¹ he) any news about it?

Dave: I don't think so. The last time I saw him (¹² he) an interview, but (¹³ he not) any definite news.

120. *Be* and *have* as main verbs (3.8 and 3.9)

Below are some sentences from science books.
  Fill in the blanks with the correct forms of *have* or *be*.

a. Many substances can exist as solids, liquids or
   gases, depending on temperature. One example
   ^{1}___ water. Water ^{2}___ a freezing point of 0°C and
   a boiling point of 100°C. This means that it ^{3}___ a
   solid below 0°C, and a gas above 100°C.
b. A pyramid ^{4}___ a solid object. The base of a
   pyramid ^{5}___ square in shape. The sides ^{6}___
   straight and flat, sloping up to a point. A cone also
   ^{7}___ a point at the top, but it ^{8}___ a circular base.
c. Blue whales ^{9}___ the largest animals in the world,
   but bootlace worms ^{10}___ the longest. The blue
   whale also ^{11}___ a long life and ^{12}___ very heavy.
   The bootlace worm's life ^{13}___ shorter and you
   could carry one in your hand.
d. Brontosaurus lived about 150 million years ago. An
   adult brontosaurus ^{14}___ a length of 20 metres or
   more, and it ^{15}___ up to 30 tonnes in weight. Why
   did it grow so large? Scientists believe that its
   large size ^{16}___ several uses, one of which ^{17}___ to
   keep the animal's temperature almost the same all
   the time.

121. *Do* as main verb (3.10)

Complete this conversation between Frank and Terry,
who live in the same student hostel. Make a suitable
verb phrase from the words in brackets, but remember
that sometimes it will be unnecessary to change *do*.

Frank: Terry, (^{1} you do) **(= are you doing)** anything
        special?
Terry: Not at the moment. (^{2} I just do) the crossword
        in today's newspaper.
Frank: (^{3} you do) your essay yet?
Terry: Yes, (^{4} I do) it this afternoon.
Frank: Well, I was wondering. (^{5} you do) me a
        favour?
Terry: It depends what it is.
Frank: Will you take a look at my essay? (^{6} I do) my
        best, but I'm still not happy with it.
Terry: Yes, of course (^{7} I do) that for you. But
        perhaps (^{8} it not do) any good. (^{9} I not often
        do) very good essays myself, you know!
Frank: Everyone says (^{10} you do) the best one last
        time, anyway.
Terry: OK. We'll discuss it in the morning. But (^{11} not
        do) any more work on it tonight, while you're
        tired. (^{12} nobody ever do) good work when
        they're feeling sleepy.

122. *Be, have,* and *do* as auxiliary verbs (3.8, 3.9 and 3.10)

As usual, Eliza Box, the famous actress, has been met at the airport by reporters with a large number of questions.

Fill in each blank with a suitable form of *be, have* or *do*. Use negative forms and short forms (*'m, n't,* etc.) where necessary.

'Miss Box, ¹___ (= **are**) you intending to stay here long?'

'No, I ²___ staying long in your beautiful country. I ³___ know exactly how long I ⁴___ staying, but probably only a few days. I ⁵___ only taking a short holiday here, you know.'

'Miss Box, there ⁶___ been stories that you ⁷___ going to get married again, to David Klein, the theatre millionaire. ⁸___ your visit here have any connection with that?'

'No, it ⁹___. Of course, David and I ¹⁰___ known each other for years, but we ¹¹___ just good friends. We ¹²___ made any plans to get married.'

'¹³___ you got any plans to meet Mr Klein while you're here?'

'No special plans. But we may meet unexpectedly at someone's party. We usually ¹⁴___.'

'Last week, Leo Spence, the theatre director, said he ¹⁵___ going to offer the part of Juliet to a younger actress – not to you, as everyone ¹⁶___ expected. Can you comment?'

'Actually, I ¹⁷___ heard anything about Mr Spence's production until three months ago. And I immediately told my agent I ¹⁸___ want the part. Nowadays I ¹⁹___ find the part of Juliet a very interesting one.'

123. *Can* and *be able to* expressing ability (3.11)

The editor of a newspaper likes his journalists to use *can* and *could* instead of *be able to* wherever possible, because they take less space. A young journalist has been told to rewrite this article.

Decide which of the expressions *in italics* can be changed, and then change them.

WILL IT BE BENDER'S DAY OF GLORY?

¹ *Is* Andrew Bender *able to win*? That's the question millions of tennis fans are asking before today's championship final against Tim Mackintosh. Too often this year Bender just ² *hasn't been able to win* the really big matches. But in his last match against Peter Collins, Bender ³ *was able to show* us the kind of tennis no other living player ⁴ *is able to equal.*

At his best, Bender ⁵ *is able to beat* any player in the world. Even when he was a junior he ⁶ *was able to hit* the ball harder than players several years older, and in 1985 ⁷ *was able to win* the Under 18 World Championship. But even in those days he ⁸ *wasn't always able to control* his shots. Sadly, Bender doesn't always play as we know he ⁹ *is able to.* And if he isn't at his best this afternoon, he certainly ¹⁰ *won't be able to beat* Mackintosh.

One thing is certain – both players ¹¹ *are able to play* the kind of tennis others ¹² *are only able to dream of.* I, for one, ¹³ *am not able to wait* to see it!

124. *Can* for possibility, permission, requests and conclusions (3.11, 3.13.1 and 3.17.3)

After a day's skiing some teenagers are waiting to go home because one of the group is missing.

Complete their conversation by using the words in brackets together with *can, can't, could* or *couldn't*. Follow these with *have* + past participle where necessary.

Rudi: Sam isn't here. Where (¹ he be)? **(= can he be?)**

Tracy: He was with us when we came back to the Ski Centre. So (² he be) far away.

Taro: (³ I go) and look for him, if you like.

Rudi: Hold on a moment, Taro. (⁴ someone else see) him.

Karen: (⁵ he go) to the cafe for a sandwich.

Bill: No, (⁶ he do) that. It closed half an hour ago.

Rudi: I suppose (⁷ he still be) in the changing room. Taro, (⁸ you go) and look for him there? I'll go and check the souvenir shop, and (⁹ the rest of you stay) here.
(Sam appears)

Rudi: Well, hello, Sam. Where on earth have you been?

Sam: I've been looking for Tracy. Tracy, (¹⁰ you wait) for me? I said I was going to buy some postcards.

Tracy: Did you? I'm so sorry. (¹¹ I be) listening.

Rudi: Well, never mind. We're all here now. So (¹² we all get) on the bus.

125. *May/be allowed to* expressing permission (3.12)

In the early nineteenth century Oliver Twist lived in a home for very poor children. The manager of the home was not kind, and when the children asked him for anything, he usually refused. Here are some of their requests:

1. Oliver was hungry one day and wanted more food.
2. The boys wanted to play football sometimes.
3. Oliver wanted to write to his uncle.
4. Oliver wanted to wear extra clothes on cold days.
5. The boys wanted to have a party at Christmas.
6. The boys wanted to run in the park sometimes.
7. Oliver wanted to keep a pet mouse.

But when they asked about these things, the answers were:

1. No.
2. Yes, for ten minutes every Saturday.
3. Yes, once a month.
4. No.
5. No.
6. Yes, on one afternoon every month.
7. No.

(a) Make dialogues for each question and answer, using *may*.

Example:
1. Oliver: May I have more food, please?
   Manager: No, you may not.

(b) Years later, Oliver wrote about his days in the home. He described conditions, using *allowed to*. What did he write? Make sentences for each of the dialogues you wrote above.

Example:
1. I was not allowed to have more food.

126. *May* and *might* expressing possibility (3.12)

Della has invited some people to dinner at her home. As she waits for them to arrive she feels rather excited and anxious.

Read what she thinks below. Then complete the sentences, using the words in brackets together with *may/might* or *may/might have* + past participle.

1. Linda should be here by now. But she (get stuck) **(= may have got stuck)** in a traffic jam.
2. I forgot how careful Aunt Sally is about what she eats. She (not eat) spicy food.
3. I wonder what time Carol will arrive. She said she (be late).
4. Daniel should be coming, but I haven't heard anything from him. He (not receive) my invitation.
5. I wrote a letter to Frank, but perhaps he didn't get it. One of his friends thought he (move) to a new house.
6. Betty said she'd be early, but she isn't here yet. She (lose) the directions I gave her.
7. I left a message for Diana. I wonder why she didn't phone back? She (not want) to speak to me after our quarrel last year.
8. It's quite possible Denis will be late. He (not be able) to get away from the office in time.
9. I'd better go and check the soup. It (boil over) by now.
10. Perhaps Guy won't be able to go back to London tonight. He (have to) stay the night at a hotel.

127. *Must* and *have to* expressing obligation and necessity (3.13.1 and 3.13.2)

Les is going to take a group of young people on a hill-walking holiday. He is telling them some things they must know before they set out.

Complete his explanations with a suitable form of *must* or *have to*. Sometimes more than one answer is possible.

'Well, before we set out, there are some things you ¹___ remember. So will everyone listen carefully, please?

The main thing is, we ²___ all stay together when we are on the hills. Last year, we ³___ call out the mountain rescue team, when someone in the group got lost. We found him, but I ⁴___ apologize to a lot of people for the trouble we'd caused. So on this trip we ⁵___ show people that we know how to look after ourselves. And of course, everybody ⁶___ have the right clothes and equipment. You've got a list of what to bring.

Now, about transport. The bus is going to pick us up from here tomorrow morning at 6.30, so we ⁷___ be here by then. It's a long trip to the hills, and so the driver won't be happy if he ⁸___ wait for anybody.

Now, Ruth and Jimmy, I know that you ⁹___ come home early, and that your friends are going to collect you by car. That's OK. And Kenny, you ¹⁰___ drop out because you ¹¹___ go to an interview. Sorry you can't come, but I hope you get the job. We ¹²___ arrange another trip sometime, and you can come on that.'

128. Negative forms of *must, have to* and *need* (3.13)

Complete the conversations with a negative form of *must, have to* or *need*, in the correct tense. Sometimes more than one answer is possible.

(a) *Phil is going for a job interview soon. He's talking to Jim about it.*

Phil: I wish I ^{1}____ go for this interview.
Jim: Why? You'll be all right.
Phil: It's all very well for you to talk, Jim. You ^{2}____ go for the interview.
Jim: Well, the main thing is, you ^{3}____ get too worried about it. I'm sure you ^{4}____ answer any really difficult questions.
Phil: Maybe not. But the silly thing is, I'm not even sure I want the job now!
Jim: Well, that's something you can find out. After all, you ^{5}____ take the job, even if it's offered to you.

(b) *A manager is talking to an employee.*

Manager: John, you don't look at all well.
John: I think I've got some kind of flu.
Manager: Well, you ^{6}____ come in this morning, really. We aren't very busy. And people ^{7}____ come to work if they don't feel well.
John: Yes, I know I ^{8}____ come to work. But I have an important report to write. I felt that I ^{9}____ leave it any longer.
Manager: OK. See how you feel today. But you ^{10}____ come to work tomorrow if you still feel bad. Just take the day off.

129. *Must* and *can't* expressing conclusions (3.13.1 and 3.11.2)

Rose and Jack are discussing their new neighbours and trying to work out what sort of people they are.

Complete their conversation, using the verbs in brackets together with *must/must have* or *can't/can't have*.

Rose: He (^{1} be) rich. There's a big Volvo parked outside the gate.
Jack: But it (^{2} belong) to him. I saw him driving a Mazda last night.
Rose: Look – there's a woman getting out of a Mazda now, Jack! She (^{3} be) his wife.
Jack: That means they (^{4} have) a car each. They (^{5} have) plenty of money. I wonder where they were living before they moved here.
Rose: They (^{6} come) from Scotland. The removal van had the name of a Glasgow company on it.
Jack: Well, he (^{7} live) there all his life. He talks like a Londoner. I heard him shouting at the van driver.
Rose: I wonder if they'll like the house. They (^{8} hear) about the trouble the Wilsons had with it. Otherwise they wouldn't have bought it.
Jack: Yes. The Wilsons (^{9} laugh) like anything when they finally sold that house!
(There is a knock at the door. Jack answers it.)
Jack: Hello. You (^{10} be) our new neighbours. Come in.
Neigh-bour: No thanks, I won't come in. But I wonder if you can help us? We (^{11} get) all the keys of the house, because we can't open the door of one room. There's a funny noise coming from inside it. The Wilsons (^{12} leave) something in there . . .

130. *Shall* expressing offers or suggestions (3.14.1)

Make the question which goes in front of each answer, using the words in the box.

Shall	I we	dance? go to visit your parents this weekend? meet for lunch? have some coffee? post these letters for you? do the washing up?

Answers:
1. Yes, please, if there's any warm water.
2. You have some if you like. I shan't.
3. Let's wait until there are some more people on the floor.
4. I'm afraid I can't. I have to be in the office from twelve till two.
5. Yes, perhaps we ought to. We haven't seen them for several weeks now.
6. No, it's all right, I have to go and buy some stamps anyway.

131. *Should* (3.14.1)

Linda is phoning her sister Carol. Part of their conversation is about Carol's boyfriend, Tony.

Complete the conversation with statements or questions using *should, shouldn't, should have* or *shouldn't have*, together with the correct form of the verb in brackets.

Linda: Hello, Carol. (¹ I really phone) **(= I should really have phoned)** earlier, to thank you for dinner last night. It was marvellous! (² you not take) so much trouble.

Carol: Oh, you know how I enjoy cooking. By the way, you left your glasses behind.

Linda: Did I? I'm always doing that. (³ I really look after) my things better.

Carol: I had a letter from Tony this morning. It says he's coming back to Britain on the 6th.

Linda: The 6th? But that's today! (⁴ he not arrive) by now?

Carol: No, there's a flight this evening so (⁵ he be) on that. Do you think (⁶ I go) and meet him at the airport? Or (⁷ I wait) and see if he phones?

Linda: I think (⁸ you wait). (⁹ he not really expect) you to meet him if he doesn't tell you the flight number.

Carol: I suppose you're right. His letter is a bit worrying really. He says he's got money problems.

Linda: That doesn't surprise me. He lent a lot of money to his American friends, didn't he? (¹⁰ he not trust) them so easily. (¹¹ he ask) them for some kind of guarantee.

132. *Ought to* (3.14.2)

(a) Say what the people in the pictures *ought to (do)* or *ought to have (done)*. These ideas are provided to help you; they are *not* in the same order as the pictures.

give up his seat; take a map with him; stop the game; cancel her order; close the window; check his brakes; put out her cigarette; fill the radiator with water

Example:
1. They ought to have closed the window.

(b) Now make negative sentences, using *ought not to (do)* or *oughtn't to have (done)*. You may use these ideas, which are again in a different order from the pictures.

start smoking; drive with an empty radiator; go on holiday without telling the newsagent; let the game continue; set out without a map; let the lady stand; start out without checking his brakes; leave the window open

Example:
1. They oughtn't to have left the window open.

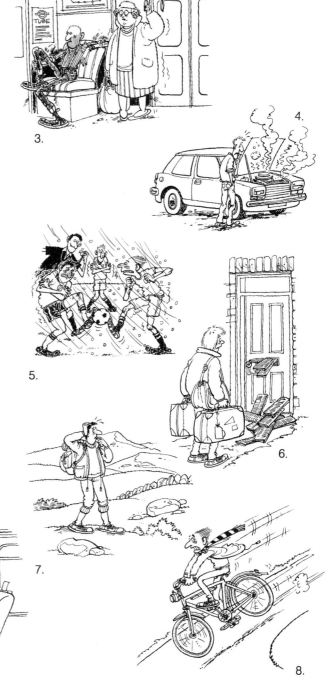

3.

4.

5.

6.

7.

1.

2.

8.

133. *Will/would* (3.15)

Here is an extract from 'The Spy who Sat by the Fire' by John Diamond.

Fill in each blank in the story with one of the words in the box. More than one may be suitable sometimes.

```
will   won't   'd   would   wouldn't
will not   would not   'll
```

Tarrant spoke harshly: '[1]___ you tell me where Parker is? Or [2]___ you prefer it if I told your masters about the game you've been playing?'

Kramer sighed. He [3]___ tell Tarrant anything unless he was sure of getting something in return. Almost wearily he said, 'Oh dear, Mr. Tarrant. You people [4]___ use threats to get what you want.' He paused. 'But if I were you, I [5]___ bother to tell my masters anything. If you did, they [6]___ only laugh at you. They know about my game, you see. In fact, it was they who suggested it.'

Tarrant looked amazed. Kramer's voice was friendly, polite. '[7]___ you sit down, have some coffee, and relax?' he said. 'I promised you on the phone that I [8]___ discuss this matter of Parker. I [9]___ give in to threats. But maybe we can help each other.'

Tarrant sat down. 'I [10]___ like to do business with you,' he said. 'Though I don't trust you. But OK, if you tell me where Parker is, I [11]___ help you.'

'You probably [12]___ believe me,' said Kramer. 'By now Parker [13]___ be in Vienna. Later today he [14]___ have a secret meeting with Dawson, your boss.'

134. *Used to* (3.16)

In the year 2036 an old man is talking about how life has changed since he was a boy.

Some of the verb phrases in his talk can be changed to the form *used to* + infinitive. Decide which ones can be changed and change them.

At the first school I [1]*went to* (= **no change**), we [2]*did* (= **used to do**) our sums using pencil and paper. I [3]*didn't see* a pocket calculator until I [4]*was* ten years old. And as for computers – well, we [5]*read* about them in books, without knowing what they really were. Nowadays even children aged five [6]*use* them.

I remember how there [7]*were* public libraries in most towns. People [8]*got* a lot of their information from books and magazines, but now they [9]*find out* things they need to know from the information stored on computers.

Ideas about health have changed a lot, too. People [10]*smoked* cigarettes in those days. You [11]*saw* people smoking, even in the streets. There [12]*was* a lot of drinking, too. And our ideas about food are different now. I remember I [13]*ate* lots of 'junk food' – hamburgers and so on. Nowadays we [14]*eat* much healthier things.

Do you know, in those days people [15]*worked* five days a week? They [16]*went* to offices and factories to do their work, not like today, when most people [17]*carry on* their occupations at home.

135. Mixed modals (3.11. to 3.16)

Here are some people's horoscopes for next week. In
each gap two different modal verbs are offered.
Choose the one which you think makes better sense.

21 March – 20 April
Next week you (¹ may/would) see someone you
(² oughtn't to/haven't been able to) find for a very long
time. He or she is someone who (³ needn't/used to)
make you laugh a lot in the old days, but he or she
(⁴ could have changed/is allowed to change) quite a
lot since then.

24 July – 23 August
You (⁹ wouldn't/mustn't) go on as you are now, feeling
dissatisfied with yourself. Although there are many
things you (¹⁰ wouldn't/can't) do as well as you'd like,
there are other things you (¹¹ are able to/mustn't) do
very well. Fix your thoughts on these. Next week you
(¹² mightn't/should) think about things you are good
at.

21 April – 21 May
This (⁵ must/could) easily be the week when you finally
fall in love! However, the charming person you meet is
someone who (⁶ may/needs to) have no intention of
getting married. Perhaps, if it is a very young person
you meet, he or she (⁷ didn't use to/won't be allowed
to) marry by his or her parents. So you (⁸ may/must) be
careful about the relationship you enter into.

24 August – 23 September
Until recently you (¹³ wouldn't/may) have thought you
were unpopular, but now suddenly there are friends all
around you! So you (¹⁴ mustn't/won't) get much sleep
next week, as you catch up on all the exciting things
you (¹⁵ haven't been able to do/can't have done)
during the past few months. This (¹⁶ might/mustn't)
mean an expensive time for you, so remember, you
(¹⁷ shouldn't/can't) afford to spend all your savings.

Section four:

The noun phrase

136. Noun plurals (4.1.1)

Cherry Reid is a famous explorer. Below you can read part of a diary she kept when she was travelling.

Find words to fill in the gaps in her diary. The first letter of each word is given, and the pictures will help you to think of them.

Dec 11. I have walked a long way, and my <u>1</u> are tired. As I sit here, resting, I realize there just aren't enough <u>2</u> in my diary to describe this lovely place! On the hills, some <u>3</u> from the nearby village are driving their <u>4</u>. In the valley, they are ploughing with <u>5</u>, and there are also some people on the river bank, catching <u>6</u> with spears.

The <u>7</u> of the village are colourfully dressed, with red and blue <u>8</u> covering their hair. They farm small plots of land where they grow <u>9</u> and <u>10</u>. They carry their <u>11</u> on their backs all the time they are working. <u>12</u> stand outside the wooden <u>13</u> and warn the women of approaching strangers. Outside the houses the <u>14</u> are also playing. They look healthy, with perfect <u>15</u>. Some of the boys are carving toys with sharp <u>16</u>.

Life is very simple here. I have seen no <u>17</u> and the people do not even use <u>18</u> to light their fires.

1. f – – –
2. p – – – –
3. m – –
4. s – – – –
5. o – – –
6. f – – –
7. w – – – –
8. s – – – – – –
9. p – – – – – – –
10. t – – – – – –
11. b – – – – –
12. g – – – –
13. h – – – – –
14. c – – – – – – –
15. t – – – –
16. k – – – – –
17. r – – – – –
18. m – – – – – –

137. Possessive forms of nouns (4.1.2)

Martin and Ann Bone are having a new house built. Upstairs there are 7 rooms, as you can see in this plan.

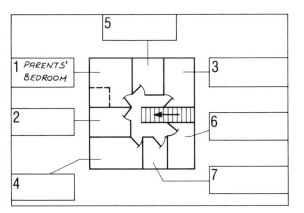

Read what a friend says about the house. Then copy the plan and label it, like the example.

1. The parents will sleep in the largest bedroom which has its own small bathroom.
2. There will be another larger bathroom for the children.
3. The eldest son, James, will have his own bedroom.
4. The twins are still very young, so they can share a bedroom.
5. There will be a playroom for the younger children, too.
6. There will be a spare room for guests.
7. Martin will have a small training room where he can do his exercises.

138. Possessive forms of nouns (4.1.2)

Martin Bone (see Exercise 137) is trying to work out when his new house will be ready to live in. He has written down the time it will take to carry out each job.
    Make further sentences from his notes.

1. drawing the plans – one month
   (= **It will be a month's work drawing the plans.**)
2. getting planning permission – three months
3. digging the ground – five days
4. laying the pipes – two days
5. building the walls – three weeks
6. putting on the roof – two weeks
7. laying the floors – a week
8. finishing off the inside – a month
9. fixing the lights – one day
10. painting the house – a week

139. Possessive with *of* and with apostrophe (4.1.2)

Here are the titles of some books in a bookshop. Change them to the possessive form with *'s* or *s'* whenever possible. If you cannot change them, leave them as they are.

1. THE TRADITIONS OF OUR COUNTRY
2. THE MOUTH OF THE HORSE
3. A GUIDE TO THE CHURCHES OF BRITAIN
4. A HAPPY CROWD OF CHILDREN
5. THE WORLD OF TOMORROW
6. TAKE IT WITH A PINCH OF SALT
7. THE WORK OF A LIFETIME
8. SONGS OF MEN WHO MARCHED AWAY
9. TALES OF WOMEN WHO CHANGED THE WORLD
10. A SURVEY OF THE INTERESTS OF STUDENTS

140. Kinds of noun (4.1.3)

A secretary at Paramco received a telex from Germany. She wanted to pass the information in the telex to various other departments. So she typed the message out in the normal way, using capital letters only where they were needed.

What did she type?

HELMUT BRAUN WILL VISIT THE UK IN MARCH, STAYING AT THE LAYTON HOTEL. AFTER SPENDING TWO WEEKS WITH PARAMCO (LONDON) HE WILL COMMENCE A TOUR OF THE PARAMCO FACTORIES IN WIGAN, LEEDS AND NEWCASTLE, ACCOMPANIED BY MR ALLEN OF THE PRODUCTION DEPARTMENT. AT THE END OF MARCH HE WILL ATTEND A TRAINING PROGRAMME ORGANIZED BY OUR PARENT COMPANY, SOLENT EXPORTS, IN THE ISLE OF WIGHT.

141. Uncountable nouns and plural nouns (4.1.4 and 4.1.5)

The headmaster of a school is giving a talk to his pupils. Some of the main points are listed below.

Choose the correct singular or plural form from the brackets in each sentence.

1. Teachers tell me that (homework/homeworks) (is/are) often handed in late. This must stop.
2. Some games are not allowed at school. In particular, (dart/darts) (is/are) forbidden, because of the danger to eyes.
3. I have noticed pupils wearing (cloth/clothes) that (is/are) not part of the official school uniform.
4. Some school (furniture/furnitures) (has/have) been damaged recently. Please be more careful.
5. The (stair/stairs) in the west wing are for the use of the (staff/staffs) only. (It/They) should not be used by pupils.
6. There will be a bring-and-buy sale next Saturday to raise money to build a swimming pool. Anyone who has (good/goods) that we can sell should bring (it/them) to school on Friday.
7. There will be a school outing to Wensleydale on 27th April. Anyone who is interested and would like (information/informations) can get (it/them) from his or her class teacher.
8. A pupil who left this school in 1980 is climbing Mount Everest this week. I hope to give you more news of this exciting event as soon as (it/they) (reach/reaches) me.
9. This announcement is for pupils who will be leaving the school at the end of this term. An officer of the Employment Service will visit the school next Thursday to give them (an/some) (advice/advices) about job opportunities.
10. The (police/polices) (has/have) found a bicycle in the pond. (It/They) would like to hear from anyone who has lost one.

142. Nationality words (4.1.6)

Identify these flags, and state the names of the countries they come from. The first letter of each country's name is given.

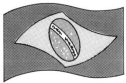

1. B_ _ _ _ _
(= Brazil)

2. C_ _ _ _ _

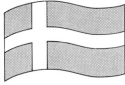

3. D_ _ _ _ _ _

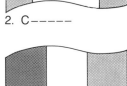

4. F_ _ _ _ _

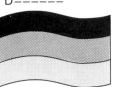

5. G_ _ _ _ _ _

6. G_ _ _ _ _

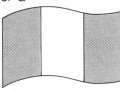

7. I_ _ _ _

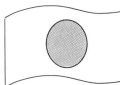

8. J_ _ _ _

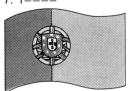

9. P_ _ _ _ _ _ _

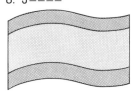

10. S_ _ _ _

11. S_ _ _ _ _ _ _ _ _

12. W_ _ _ _

143. Nationality words (4.1.6)

An international college is having an end-of-term concert. The organizer is announcing the programme.

Make the correct nationality or language word. The numbers in brackets refer to the flags in Exercise 142.

a. (3) is a country of many islands. Astrid is going to do a (3) dance for us, wearing a costume from one of the smallest islands of all.

b. Next, please welcome one of our students from (10), Carmen, who is going to play for you on her (10) guitar, and sing a song in (10).

c. You may not understand (8), but I know you will enjoy hearing Fumiko sing 'Hana', which is one of the best-known songs in (8).

d. Jean-Claude, from (4), is our next performer. He is going to recite a poem in (4), and then give us an English translation.

e. Jacques and Marie come from the part of (2) where they speak French. They are going to show us an old (2) game.

f. (7) is famous for its operas. Alberto, who comes from Naples, has chosen something from one of the best-known (7) operas, 'Aida'.

g. The (9) have always been great sailors. Francisco is going to perform a (9) sailors' dance.

h. When they play rugby in (12), the (12) crowd support their team by singing in (12). So don't be surprised if you don't understand what Huw Jones from Cardiff is now going to sing.

i. The carnivals in Rio are one of (1)'s most wonderful sights! Renata and Alicia will dance for us in real (1) costumes.

j. Vicki and Alex are from the north of (6) and it is from that part of their country that this (6) song comes.

k. Heinz and Helga are going to dance a (5) dance from the south of (5), in which the boy is trying to win the heart of the girl.

l. High in the mountains of (11), what do you do if you haven't got a telephone? Rudi is going to show us the (11) solution to this problem – yodelling!

144. The indefinite article and zero article (4.2.1 and 4.2.2)

Joy Weller is a health worker. Help her to expand these notes about patients into full sentences, as she might do when reporting to the doctor.

1. Joe Flanagan. Irish. Works as a gardener – 3 days/ week. Looking for better job.
    (= Joe Flanagan is Irish. He works as a gardener three days a week. He is looking for a better job.)
2. Mary King. Student. Has bad back and attends hospital for treatment – 1/month.
3. Bill Baker. Middle-aged labourer from coal-mining area of Scotland. Smokes cigarettes heavily – sometimes 40 cigarettes/day. Has breathing problems.
4. Liz Chalmers. Teacher. Always has stomachache. Says she needs holiday.
5. David Jordan. Businessman. Travels everywhere by taxi. Eats ½ kilo chocolate/day. Needs exercise.
6. Kate Mellors. Widow with 6-month-old baby. Living in single room. Needs financial help and advice on baby care.

145. *The* and zero article with abstract nouns (4.2.2 and 4.2.3)

Paul Herriot is making a speech in a college debate. The topic is 'History is boring'.

Complete Paul's speech by putting in the articles. Remember that sometimes you don't need to add anything (zero article).

I really can't understand [1]____ boredom which some students feel when [2]____ history is discussed. Maybe they get the wrong idea about it at school. For me, though, the subject is a most important part of [3]____ education. This is because there are some very worrying trends in [4]____ modern life. In fact, these trends could lead to [5]____ destruction of [6]____ civilization as we know it. I believe that [7]____ historical knowledge is the answer to this problem, for it increases [8]____ understanding of the process of [9]____ change. Knowing about [10]____ development of [11]____ society in previous centuries helps us to understand [12]____ society we live in now. To take another example, [13]____ twentieth century history teaches us very clearly how [14]____ competition between nations can lead to [15]____ war. We have certainly made [16]____ progress already towards understanding these matters, but not [17]____ progress we ought to have made. In my opinion, [18]____ peace and indeed [19]____ whole future of [20]____ mankind depend on [21]____ research and [22]____ careful thought. We must place a higher value on [23]____ historical research if [24]____ survival of [25]____ human race is to be assured. It's a matter of [26]____ life and [27]____ death.

146. All articles: *a/an, the* and zero article (4.2.1 to 4.2.3)

Complete these extracts from the diary of James Bone, aged 13. Either put in the correct articles (*a, an* or *the*) or, if zero article is required, leave the gap blank.

Tuesday 17 July

We did [1]____ brilliant experiment during [2]____ chemistry today. We put [3]____ substance (I forget [4]____ name of it) into [5]____ water, and it gave off [6]____ smell like [7]____ bad eggs! Denise couldn't stand it and ran out of [8]____ lab. She said she went to [9]____ girls' toilet and was sick three times. Gaining [10]____ knowledge can be [11]____ painful experience.

Wednesday 18 July

After [12]____ school I was on [13]____ duty in [14]____ library when Mr Goldby, [15]____ new teacher who teaches us [16]____ geography, came in and acted very strangely. He chose [17]____ book containing [18]____ information about [19]____ spy scandals and went off into [20]____ dark corner of [21]____ room to read it. I pretended to be dusting [22]____ shelves and gradually crept towards him. But when I got close he shut [23]____ book quickly and went red in [24]____ face. Is Mr Goldby [25]____ secret agent for [26]____ foreign power? I must ask Denise to help me find out. She's good at [27]____ finding out [28]____ secrets.

Thursday 19 July

Today school finished for [29]____ summer holidays. Before we left [30]____ school I put [31]____ note in Denise's bag. It said, 'I'm starting [32]____ big spy hunt tomorrow and I need [33]____ help from you, because you're [34]____ best detective I know. Can we meet early in [35]____ morning at [36]____ entrance to [37]____ shopping centre in [38]____ Duke Street? Bring [39]____ camera, if you can. Don't worry, I'll pay for [40]____ film.
James
PS. [41]____ future of [42]____ nation may be in our hands! We must act in [43]____ time!'

147. Adjectives used as nouns (4.3.2)

Senator Wilson has made some notes for a speech. Complete them by adding *the* in front of the adjective in brackets wherever possible. Otherwise add *people* after the adjective.

1. We must give more help to (poor) **(= the poor)**, even if this means that some (rich) **(= some rich people)** have to pay very heavy taxes.
2. Last week a group of twenty (unemployed) came to see me. I began to realize how difficult life is for (unemployed).
3. We should also look at the problems of (young). The present government is spending less on education, with the result that the standards of education of our (young) have fallen.
4. But it is not only (young) who are suffering. The situation of many (old) is desperate also. And every society must help (old).
5. It is our responsibility to look after (old), (weak) and (sick). Recently life has become harder for those (sick) who do not have enough money to pay for treatment and medicine.
6. Unfortunately, there are a minority of (greedy) in our society who care only about themselves.
7. But we must stand up against such (selfish).
8. All (decent) should reject the arguments of (heartless or uncaring).

148. Comparison of adjectives with pronoun *one* (4.3.3 and 4.3.5)

Sandra is going to a wedding and needs to buy a lot of new clothes. But she is very hard to please.

Complete her conversation with the shop assistant by adding a suitable adjective and either *one* or *ones*. Also fill in *a/an*, as necessary.

Assistant: Here's a light-coloured dress that might suit you.

Sandra: No, it's too expensive. Have you got [1]____?
(= a cheaper one)

Assistant: Sorry. That's all we've got left in your size. How about this skirt?

Sandra: It's too long. Haven't you got [2]____?

Assistant: There's this one, but as you see, it's dark-coloured.

Sandra: No, that's no use. I really must have [3]____. Let me see some shoes instead.

Assistant: Here are some in the latest fashion.

Sandra: Maybe. But the heels are too low. I need [4]____, because I'm not very tall.

Assistant: This pair has got high heels.

Sandra: Yes, but they don't look very expensive. I want [5]____.

Assistant: I'm afraid that's the best I can do. Is there anything else I can show you?

Sandra: Yes, I'd like some gloves. I've got these short ones for everyday wear. But I need [6]____ for the wedding.

Assistant: Would you like to try these?

Sandra: But they're so big! I need [7]____.

Assistant: Sorry, madam, I haven't any others.

Sandra: (*thinks*) This isn't a good shop at all. I'll go to [8]____.

Assistant: (*thinks*) What an unpleasant person you are! I hope the next customer is [9]____.

149. Comparison of adjectives with pronoun *one* (4.3.3 and 4.3.5)

Four young people wanted to compare the cars they had bought, so they made this chart.

The example shows what they said about Bengt's car. Make similar statements about the cars bought by Ingrid, Sven and Diana. Use the adjectives given in the table.

Example:
Bengt's car is the most expensive and most powerful one. But it is also the least modern one.

	Size of boot (cu ft)	Year made	Size of engine (cc)	Max. speed (kph)	Km per litre	Price paid	Practicality
Bengt	14	1980	2000	148	50	6,000	***
Ingrid	10	1984	1500	164	48	5,500	*
Sven	16	1982	1800	152	55	4,500	****
Diana	12	1985	950	130	80	5,000	**
	spacious	modern	powerful	fast/slow	economical	expensive	practical

150. Special predicative uses of adjectives (4.3.4)

Ann has been married for several years. She is looking at old photographs and writing comments on them. Complete each comment by choosing the correct words in brackets.

1. When I first met Karl he always dressed so (smart/smartly).

2. But after a month or two he started to look (awful/awfully)!

3. And when I took him home for the first time he behaved (dreadful/dreadfully).

4. Karl always looked (good/well) on the tennis court, but he never played (good/well).

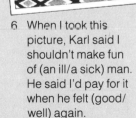

5. This meal we had together in the south of France tasted (delicious/deliciously).

6. When I took this picture, Karl said I shouldn't make fun of (an ill/a sick) man. He said I'd pay for it when he felt (good/well) again.

7. On our wedding day the church bells sounded (wonderful/wonderfully), and the organist played the wedding march (loud/loudly) as we left the church.

8. As for the weather, our wedding day seemed (perfect/perfectly) – then the rain came down!

151. Comparison of adjectives (4.3.5)

Here are the marks four students got in a recent English test.

Name	Listening	Speaking	Reading	Writing
Pedro	43%	51%	86%	62%
Susanna	62%	64%	73%	49%
Monika	57%	73%	69%	55%
Marcel	54%	48%	78%	64%

(a) Complete the sentences with the correct form of *good* or *bad*.

1. Pedro is ____ at listening.
   (= Pedro is the worst at listening.)
2. But he is ____ at reading.
3. Susanna is ____ at writing.
4. But she is ____ at listening.
5. Monika is ____ at speaking.
6. But she is ____ at reading.
7. Marcel is ____ at speaking.
8. But he is ____ at writing.

(b) Make five more sentences like this example:
   Monika is better than Marcel at listening.

(c) Then make five more sentences like this different example:
   Marcel is better at listening than speaking.

152. Comparison of adjectives (4.3.5 and 4.3.6)

Match each picture with the appropriate words in boxes A and B to make 9 sentences.

A	B
fast	animal on land
popular	tree in the world
high	planet from Earth
heavy	ship in the world
distant	sport in the world
tall	bridge in England
long	place on Earth
big	bird in the world
cold	mountain in the world

1. The peregrine falcon   **(= The peregrine falcon is the fastest bird in the world.)**

2. The South Pole

3. Pluto

4. The African elephant

5. The Humber Bridge

6. Football

7. The 'Seawise Giant'

8. Everest

9. The Californian redwood

153. Forms of adverb (4.4.1)

Luke Hope has written a mystery story, but feels now that it needs more adverbs.

Choose the more appropriate of the two adjectives in each set of brackets, and then make its adverb form.

Something bumped ([1] funny/loud) (**= loudly**) on the stairs outside my room. I had been working ([2] heavy/busy) and the noise disturbed me. 'Who is it?' I cried ([3] irritable/happy). There was no answer. I went to the door and opened it ([4] light/quick). And then I saw it! A black figure was coming towards me ([5] amusing/slow but steady) down the stairs. Although the face was in shadow, I saw that it was grinning ([6] merry/horrible) and pointing a finger at me ([7] accusing/wonderful).

'Go away!' I cried ([8] fearful/laughing). But it came nearer, and its red eyes looked at me ([9] soft/piercing). I struck ([10] hard/rich) at it with my fist, but an iron hand reached out and held my wrist ([11] firm/soft).

The monster began to drag me ([12] clumsy/polite) up the stairs. Thinking my last hour had come, I struggled ([13] angry/desperate), but it still held me ([14] gentle/tight).

Then I saw Richard, the new office boy, at the top of the stairs. Seeing my danger, he came ([15] heroic/nice) to the rescue. Then the monster disappeared as ([16] brave/sudden) as it had come.

154. Adverbs similar to adjectives (4.4.1 and 4.4.2)

Here is part of a commentary on a Grand Prix race.

Complete the sentences with an adverb or comparative adverb formed from the adjectives *good*, *hard* or *fast*.

Julio Spinetti is going very [1]___ and so is Ricki Leiter. And Foreman in third place is doing [2]___ than in any previous race this season. And now I've got Spinetti's time for the lap – 5 minutes 15 seconds! He's really driving [3]___! In fact, he's finished that lap two seconds [4]___ than the previous one. And now I can see Lacombe in fourth place. He's trying to overtake Foreman. No, he hasn't done it yet. He didn't try very [5]___ that time, but he's sure to try [6]___ next time he sees a chance. He probably thinks he can do [7]___ in the straight.

155. Personal pronouns and possessive pronouns (4.5.1 to 4.5.3)

Teresa Murphy is writing a letter to her sister Bridget.
  Choose the correct form in each set of brackets to complete these sentences from the letter.

1. (It/It's/Its) wonderful to have a home of (ours/our/us) own at last.
2. We haven't got all (our/ours) furniture yet, but we've borrowed some things from some friends of (us/our/ours).
3. This is a very quiet place. Where we were living before I risked (my/the) life every time I crossed the road!
4. Martin is very happy because he now has (his/an/the) own workroom.
5. But he's worried about the car. There's a garage for (it/its/it's), but at the moment (it/its/it's) full of junk.
6. Nobody seems to know who part of the garden belongs to. We think (it's/its) (us/our/ours), but the neighbours think (it's/its) (them/their/theirs).
7. Martin says we can still afford to have a holiday this summer, but I don't believe (it/so).
8. Anyway, I don't really mind if we don't go anywhere this year. As (it says/one says/they say), 'there's no place like home'.
9. Now some family news: James is going to play for the school football team. At least he hopes (it/so).
10. Unfortunately, he fell off his bike last week and hurt (his/the) leg.
11. Thanks for your card on my birthday, even though it reminded me it was my thirtieth! Of course, it will soon be (your/yours) too, won't it?
12. And how is Michael? Has he still got that funny old car of (him/his)?

156. Pronouns ending in *-self* or *-selves* (4.5.4)

Here are some sentences which a teacher said to her class.
  Complete each of them by putting the correct pronoun ending in *-self* or *-selves* in each gap.

1. Don't copy from your neighbour, Betty. Do the exercise ___! (= **Do the exercise yourself!**)
2. John, let Bill and Joe get on with their work by ___. They don't need your help.
3. Tomorrow will be sports day, as you know. Don't bring any food. The school will provide plenty of sandwiches, and we can all help ___.
4. The school holidays begin the day after tomorrow. I hope you will all enjoy ___.
5. Look at Betty! She has just cut ___ with her scissors! Now you see how careful you must be.
6. Thank you, Jimmy. But it's all right, I can clean the blackboard ___ this time.
7. Here's a picture of a poor little dog. It's walking on only three legs. It must have hurt ___.
8. Do you know the story of the man who was so lonely that he sent a postcard to ___?
9. Sarah, perhaps you could look after the new girl during the break? She's all by ___, with no one to talk to.

157. Reciprocal pronouns (4.5.5)

A teacher has problems with her class and is thinking about moving students to different seats. She has made this sketch.

Make a sentence about each pair of students, like the examples. Notice that you will sometimes have to add a preposition.

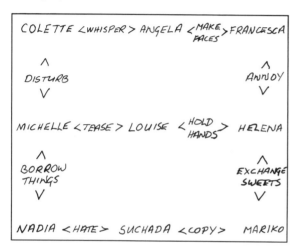

1. Colette – Angela:
   (= Colette and Angela whisper to each other.)
2. Colette – Michelle:
   (= Colette and Michelle disturb each other.)
3. Angela – Francesca.
4. Francesca – Helena.
5. Helena – Louise.
6. Louise – Michelle.
7. Michelle – Nadia.
8. Nadia – Suchada.
9. Suchada – Mariko.
10. Mariko – Helena.

How many of your sentences can you rewrite like this example?
Louise and Helena hold *each other's* hands.

158. *This, these, that, those* (4.5.6)

Meg has brought some holiday photos home for Mark to look at.

Complete their conversation by putting *this, these, that* or *those* into each gap.

Meg: Look, Mark. ___¹ are the photos from our holiday.

Mark: Oh, good. What's ___² one?

Meg: ___³ was the cafe near the beach. Remember? And ___⁴ was when we were going swimming.

Mark: Yes, I remember. Mm, I like ___⁵ one. Surely ___⁶ are the German girls who were staying at our hotel?

Meg: No. ___⁷ aren't the German girls. The girls at our hotel were Dutch. ___⁸ German girls we met were staying in ___⁹ hotel near the post office.

Mark: Oh yes, that's right. They were among all ___¹⁰ tourists from Berlin.

Meg: ___¹¹ one hasn't come out very well. But I think it's ___¹² hill we climbed on the day we arrived.

Mark: Yes, I'd like to climb ___¹³ hill again.

Meg: Well, we can't go on any more holidays ___¹⁴ year. All our money's gone!

159. *Some, any, one, no* (4.5.9, 4.5.10.1 and 4.5.11)

Jean and David have come home after a day out.
Read their conversation and fill in each blank with *some, any, one* or *no*.

David: I'm hungry. Is there ^{1}___ food in the house?

Jean: There might be ^{2}___ eggs in the fridge. You could make an omelette.

David: OK. I'll make ^{3}___. And I'll see if there are ^{4}___ vegetables.

Jean: You might find ^{5}___ potatoes. You could fry them.

David: Yes. Shall I cook ^{6}___ food for you too?

Jean: No, thanks. But if there's ^{7}___ tea left, I'll have ^{8}___.

David: Sorry. There's ^{9}___ tea left. But if you like I'll get ^{10}___ more from the village store.

Jean: Yes, please. And while you're there, could you get ^{11}___ biscuits? And a loaf of bread? I thought we had ^{12}___, but now I see we haven't ^{13}___ bread at all.

David: I'd better get ^{14}___ fruit as well. We don't seem to have ^{15}___.

Jean: And we've ^{16}___ drinks in the house, so buy ^{17}___ lemonade as well.

David: How many bottles?

Jean: Just ^{18}___.

160. Compounds of *some, any* and *no* (4.5.10.2 and 4.5.11)

Here is part of an advertisement for a new video about a terrible monster.
Fill in each blank with one of the words from the box. Notice that you will need to use some words more than once.

anyone	no one (×2)	someone
anything	nothing (×2)	something
anywhere (×2)	nowhere	somewhere
		somehow

^{1}___, on the edge of a city, a creature is waiting. The creature is more terrible than ^{2}___ you have ever dreamed of in your worst nightmares. It is a creature that has ^{3}___ survived from the age of the dinosaurs. There is ^{4}___ you can hide from the monster. It has the power to strike ^{5}___, at any time. The authorities are alarmed, because ^{6}___ can find any defence against this terrible creature. ^{7}___, not even bombs, can harm it.

But wait! Perhaps there is ^{8}___ who can save the city, a hero whose real name is known to ^{9}___. He calls himself Captain Zero. Yet even Captain Zero can do ^{10}___ against the monster without the magic sword Elonon, which has not been seen ^{11}___ on Earth for two thousand years. If ^{12}___ can find the sword, it is Captain Zero. But will his powers be enough?

Find out by watching *Captain Zero and the Green Terror*.

This video is ^{13}___ you simply must not miss!

161. *Each, every, everything, everybody, all* (4.5.12 and 4.5.13)

Caleb Dawson is 100 years old. He is remembering a school trip he made soon after he started school.

Fill in the gaps below with *each, every, everything, everybody* or *all*. Sometimes more than one answer is possible.

One day ¹___ year, ²___ the children in the school went on an outing. The teachers were busy for days before that, for ³___ had to be prepared beforehand. You know, in those days there were no buses. So ⁴___ travelled by train, or by horse and cart. Anyway, we ⁵___ got on carts outside the school. And as ⁶___ of us got on, we were given an apple to eat on the journey. Then the carts took us to the station. When I started school I had never even seen a train. So ⁷___ was new to me.

The teachers had to count ⁸___ child as we got onto the train to make sure ⁹___ was there. At last the train set off and two hours later we reached the seaside. We had tremendous fun ¹⁰___ day. ¹¹___ ran races, and ¹²___ of us got a prize. It didn't matter if you won or not. I think the prize was some sweets, and we had a bar of chocolate ¹³___.

The teachers were kept really busy. ¹⁴___ of them had a special job. One looked after the games, another the cooking, and so on. I remember, we ¹⁵___ had soup for lunch and ¹⁶___ had enough. You remember days like that ¹⁷___ your life.

162. *Not much, not many, (not) enough, plenty of, a few, only a little* (4.5.14 and 4.5.15)

Ann is planning the week's meals for her family and has made notes of what food she has got and what she needs.

Make sentences about the amounts of different kinds of food Ann has. Begin each sentence with either *She's got* or *She hasn't got*. Make:

a. 2 sentences containing *not much*
b. 2 sentences containing *not many*
c. 1 sentence containing *plenty of*
d. 1 sentence containing *enough* and 1 with *not enough*
e. 2 sentences containing *a few*
f. 1 sentence containing *only a little*

Example:
a. She hasn't got much bread.

kind of food	quantity I have	quantity I need
potatoes	½ kg	400–500 g
flour	100 g	100–150 g
grapes	¼ kg	1 or 2 kg
onions	4	3 or 4
cooking oil	⅒ litre	½ litre
bread	½ loaf	2 loaves
butter	1 kg	¼ kg
rice	400 g	less than ½ kg
apples	2	5 or 6
carrots	3 kg	1 kg

163. Numbers and fractions (4.5.16.1 and 4.5.16.4)

A student at an international school is going to give a talk about his country, Pacifica.

Look at the notes he has made and complete the sentences from his talk (using words, not figures).

PACIFICA TODAY
Population: about 2,000,000
Capital city: Port Antonio (pop. 50,276)
Annual rainfall: 0.08 cm (in north); 210 cm (in south)
¾ of people live on coast
⅓ can't read or write
Number of cinemas: 44
Lowest temperature ever recorded: 0.5°C
Highest temperature ever recorded: 34.7°C
Further information:phone Pacifican Tourist Office
           (Kensington 41025)

---

1. The population of Pacifica is ____.
2. ____ of the population live on the coast.
3. ____ of the population can't read or write.
4. There are ____ cinemas in Pacifica.
5. The lowest temperature ever recorded was ____.
6. The highest temperature ever recorded was ____.
7. ____ people live in the capital, Port Antonio.
8. The annual rainfall is ____ centimetres in the north and ____ centimetres in the south.
9. If you want any further information you could phone the Pacifican Tourist Office. The number is Kensington ____.

164. Ordinal numbers (4.5.16.2)

Look at these final positions of the best British cyclists in last year's Cycling Championship.

Make sentences like the example for the other cyclists.

Example:
Robert Fuller came third.

Cyclist	Position
Robert Fuller	3
James Reid	12
Gary Bell	21
Kevin Woodfall	42
Chris Templeton	55
Lewis Hart	100

165. Expressions of frequency, fractions (4.5.16.3 and 4.5.16.4)

The students at the Hardgraft School of English like to go to the beach. Look at this graph. It shows the number of times students in a class of 24 go to the beach each week.

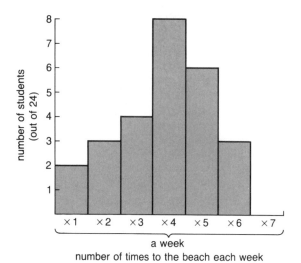

number of times to the beach each week

Use the figures above to make sentences.

Example:
An/One eighth of the students go to the beach six times a week.

166. Dates (4.5.17)

Here is information about the births and deaths of some famous Britons and Americans. Note that the information about Americans is given in the American sequence and the information about British people in the British sequence.

Make a sentence about each of them like the example.

1. William Wordsworth
   b. 7/4/1770 d. 23/4/1850 (British poet)

(= **William Wordsworth was born on 7th April 1770 and died on 23rd April 1850.**)

2. Queen Victoria
   b. 24/5/1819 d. 22/1/1901
   (British Queen)

3. Abraham Lincoln
   b. 2/12/1809 d. 4/14/1865
   (American President)

5. John Lennon
   b. 9/10/1940 d. 8/12/1980
   (British songwriter)

7. Marilyn Monroe
   b. 6/1/1926 d. 8/5/1962
   (American film actress)

4. Mary Wollstonecraft
   b. 27/4/1759 d. 10/9/1797
   (British champion of the rights
   of women)

6. Martin Luther King
   b. 1/15/1929 d. 4/4/1968
   (American civil rights leader)

8. Charlie Chaplin
   b. 16/4/1889 d. 25/12/1977
   (British comedian)

167. Time of day (4.5.17)

Look at the clock faces below. Write out the time on
each clock in two ways.

1.   AM

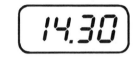

2.

(**= Ten past eleven
in the morning/
11.10 a.m.**)

3.   PM

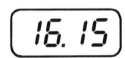

4.

5.   6.   AM

7.   8.

            PM

168. Prepositions of time (4.5.18.2)

Jack is talking to his boss. Put the correct preposition
into each blank in their conversation.

Roger: Well, Jack. How long have you been with the
            company now?

Jack: [1]____ ten years. But as you know, I've only
            been working in the Sales Department [2]____
            the beginning of the year.

Roger: Yes, I remember you joined the Sales
            Department [3]____ January. And we recognize
            that you have done a lot of good work. Would
            you like to attend the sales conference [4]____
            July? It's in Cairo this year.

Jack: That would be marvellous! What date is it
            exactly?

Roger: It begins [5]____ 22nd July. It goes on then [6]____
            nearly a week, [7]____ 28th July. You could be
            back here [8]____ the end of the month.

Jack: Well, I'd very much like to go then. Thanks.

Roger: [9]____ the conference I'd like you to take notes
            of the main decisions. Then, [10]____ the
            conference, when you get back, I'd like you
            to send me a report.

Jack: Yes, of course. I'll do that. I'd better start
            making travel arrangements.

Roger: Well, that shouldn't be difficult. There's a
            convenient flight to Cairo every Sunday [11]____
            11.15 a.m.

Jack: OK. I suppose I'd better buy a summer suit. It
            must be hot in Cairo [12]____ summer.

Roger: Oh, one other thing. There's a meeting of all
            sales staff [13]____ Friday this week, [14]____
            10.00 a.m. [15]____ 3.00 p.m. You'll be there,
            won't you?

Jack: Yes, of course.

169. Prepositions of place and direction (4.5.18.1)

The Mackenzies are very fond of animals. Look at the picture below and complete the sentences. Choose from the prepositions in the box. You can use some of them more than once.

above	behind	into	over
across	between	off	round
after	by	on	through
against	from	opposite	to
along	in front of	out of	under
among	in the middle of	outside	up

1. There is a bookcase _____ the wall, and a mouse running _____ the top of the bookcase. A cat is running _____ the mouse.
2. There is a fishtank _____ the table, with one large fish _____ a crowd of little fish.
3. One monkey is climbing _____ a curtain; another monkey is leaning _____ the fishtank, dipping its paw _____ the water.
4. There is a picture of a horse _____ the chair; the horse is jumping _____ a fence.
5. Mr Mackenzie is walking _____ the room, _____ the table _____ the bookcase.
6. Two dogs are chasing each other _____ the table.
7. Mrs Mackenzie is standing _____ the mirror. There is a picture of Grandfather Mackenzie _____ the mirror.
8. There is a birdcage _____ the cupboard and the window, and a snake crawling _____ the cupboard.
9. Young Master Mackenzie is _____ the house, looking _____ the window _____ the house.
10. A rabbit is jumping _____ the table, which stands _____ the room, _____ the lamp.

170. Various prepositions and prepositional phrases (4.5.18.1 to 4.5.18.3)

Alison is telling Fiona about an unpleasant dream she had last night.

Use prepositions or prepositional phrases to complete her explanation.

Last night I was dreaming [1]___ the town where I lived when I was a child. Somehow I had arrived there [2]___ plane, although there was no airport [3]___ the town. The sun was shining brightly, but [4]___ the sunshine, I felt very cold. I met a man who looked [5]___ my husband, but he said he was my old schoolteacher. He said, 'Speaking [6]___ your teacher, I must tell you that you have no hope of passing the exam.' However, he offered to drive me [7]___ the examination room. So we went [8]___ his car, but we were late [9]___ the traffic. In fact, there was such a bad traffic jam that I had to get [10]___ the car and finish the journey [11]___ foot. But I was so late that the examiner wouldn't let me go [12]___ the examination room. I started to cry and then I woke up.

Section five:

Communicative situations

171. Greetings and closing remarks in letters (5.3)

Read each of these extracts from letters. Then choose, from the words given underneath it,
(a) the kind of person you think it could have been written to,
(b) the most suitable opening greeting, and
(c) the most suitable closing remark.

1. . . . but I'll need my bike for school on Monday, so I really can't lend it to you for a whole week. Sorry. You can have it for the weekend, though, if that's any use . . .

a) A friend	b) Dear Madam,	c) Yours sincerely,
A stranger	Dear Miss Wright,	Yours faithfully,
A customer	Dear Sally,	Love,

2. . . . Unfortunately, the book you require is now out of print. However, it may be possible to obtain a second-hand copy for you. Would you kindly let us know . . .

a) A friend	b) Dear Jim,	c) Yours sincerely,
A relative	Dear Mr Wright,	Yours faithfully,
A customer	Dear Sir,	Love,

3. . . . For some time now I have been trying unsuccessfully to buy a copy of Johnson's 'Seven Seas', and wonder if perhaps you have one in your shop. If so, I wonder . . .

a) A friend	b) Dear William,	c) Yours sincerely,
A relative	Dear Sir or Madam,	Yours faithfully,
Someone in business	Dear Sir,	Love,

172. Inviting people (5.5)

Which of the phrases or clauses (a – i) complete an invitation if they are put into the gap marked X?

'__X__ a week at our cottage in the south of France(?)'

a. Can you afford enough money to spend
b. Maybe you'd like to spend
c. How about spending
d. What made you think you could spend
e. Would you like to spend
f. Wouldn't it have been nice to have spent
g. What about inviting me to spend
h. Do you mind very much having to spend
i. If you like, you can spend

173. Requests (5.6)

Which of the phrases or clauses (a – g and a – i) complete requests, if they are put into the gaps marked X?

1. 'The room's so cold. __X__ the door?'

a. Would you mind closing
b. Do you ever close
c. Could you please close
d. Would you be so kind as to close
e. Are you close to
f. Why doesn't someone close
g. Is there someone at

2. 'I've left my handbag somewhere. __X__.'

a. I wonder if you could let me have £10?
b. Have you seen it?
c. It cost me a lot of money.
d. Could you possibly lend me £10?
e. Would you kindly lend me £10?
f. May I borrow £10 from you?
g. You haven't got £10 to spare, have you?
h. Lend me £10, will you?
i. I shan't be able to do my shopping without it.

174. Protesting and complaining (5.8)

Which of the phrases or clauses (a – i) complete a protest or complaint if they are put into the gap marked X?

' __X__ a bigger piece of cake than anyone else?'

a. Why do you always take
b. Do you want
c. Do you realize you always give yourself
d. Must you take
e. Do you mind if I give you
f. Would you mind having
g. Wouldn't you like
h. Do you really have to take
i. Is it fair that you should have

175. Declining with regrets (5.9)

Imagine that the following invitations or requests have been made by someone you know. Decline each of them with a suitable reason or excuse.

1. 'Can you come to a disco at my place on Saturday evening?'
2. 'Shall we go and have a hamburger and a cup of coffee together?'
3. 'I'm moving to a new flat on Friday. Could you come and help me move my things?'
4. 'Some of my friends are going walking in the mountains this weekend. Would you like to come too?'
5. 'I'm getting married next month. Will you be my best man/bridesmaid?'
6. 'I'm tired. Would you like to drive for a while and give me a rest?'

176. A final quiz

Here are 15 statements. Each of them is a grammar
rule in which the rule itself is broken. Correct each of
them. (If you have forgotten the rule, the reference in
brackets tells you where to look for help.)

1. Verbs has to agree with their subjects. (3.1.1)
   (= Verbs have to agree with their subjects.)
2. We put usually adverbs of frequency between
   subject and verb. (1.1.12)
3. Don't use no double negatives. (4.5.11)
4. The form of a pronoun is determined by her noun.
   (4.5.1)
5. Are you remember *Yes-No* questions are formed
   with the appropriate tense and form of *do*, unless
   the auxiliary in first position is a form of *be, have* or
   a modal? (1.2.1)
6. We don't use *either* in affirmative statements, and
   we don't use *too* in negative statements, too.
   (1.4.5)
7. The correct choice of relative pronouns depends
   on the noun who it refers to. (2.3.1)
8. We use present simple in both *if*-clause and main
   clause if the two clauses together will express an
   invariable rule. (2.3.6)
9. If there is no other auxiliary in a statement, we use
   do to make the tag-question form, aren't we?
   (1.2.4)
10. We are using present simple when we want to talk
    about habits or things which occur regularly.
    (3.2.4)
11. There are no choice about using *there is* when a
    singular noun follows. (3.8.3)
12. A nouns possessive form is made by adding 's.
    (4.1.2)
13. We must auxiliary verbs put immediately in front of
    the main verb. (1.1.5)
14. Never we can put *never* at the beginning of a
    sentence without inverting subject and verb.
    (1.1.14)
15. This sentence gives an example the student of
    how we deal with two objects in the same
    sentence. (1.1.4)

Index
by part of speech or function or word

Note that the numbers refer to the exercises (not the page numbers) in which the items occur.